TEACHING KIT

A complete curriculum teaching kit is available to accompany this book. The curriculum is titled *Women Facing Anger, Depression, Anxiety and Stress: Forbidden Causes and Emotional Solutions.* It is possible to teach the content of the resource in Sunday School classes, retreats and small groups. The kit contains the structure, outline, time sequence and learning activities, as well as many transparency patterns that allow you to make professional-quality transparencies to use as you teach.

For information on ordering this unique teaching kit, either call Christian Marriage Enrichment at 1-800-875-7560 or write to P. O. Box 2468, Orange, CA 92859-0468.

For more information on resources by Dr. Gary J. Oliver, visit www.garyandcarrieoliver.com.

A WOMAN'S FORBIDDEN EMOTION

At last, a biblically based book that encourages
women to own, express and use their anger to grow more
spiritually alive and wholly themselves.

JUDITH COUCHMAN
Author, *Designing a Woman's Life*

In *A Woman's Forbidden Emotion* Oliver and Wright offer us
women two fine gifts: encouragement to assess and value our
anger, and practical ways to deal with that anger. Of particular help
are their suggestions for dealing with abuse, harassment and marital conflict—areas in which we too often deny or dump our anger
instead of channeling it for positive changes.

NANCY GROOM
Author, *From Bondage to Bonding: Escaping Codependency*

This is a very needed and helpful book for women who are
suffering from frustration, hurt and rejection. It will greatly help
women know how to cope with their emotion of anger as
a result of these actions. I heartily recommend it!

DR. BEVERLY LAHAYE
Chairman, Concerned Women for America

A book on women and anger is long overdue.
The chapter defining anger will help to bury forever the idea that
anger is always bad and particularly unbecoming in women.

MARY ANN MAYO
Author, *Looking Good, But Feeling Bad*
Marriage and Family Counselor

A Woman's FORBIDDEN EMOTION

GARY J. OLIVER, PH.D., AND H. NORMAN WRIGHT

a division of Baker Publishing Group
Grand Rapids, Michigan

© 1993 by Gary J. Oliver and H. Norman Wright

Published by Revell
a division of Baker Publishing Group
PO Box 6287, Grand Rapids, MI 49516-6287
www.revellbooks.com

Revell edition published 2014
ISBN 978-0-8007-2559-4

Previously published by Regal Books
Moody Press edition titled *Pressure Points* published in 1993.
Servant Publications edition titled *Good Women Get Angry* published in 1995.

Printed in the United States of America

Library of Congress Cataloging Number: 2014954069

Scripture quotations labeled AMP are from the Amplified® Bible, copyright © 1954, 1958, 1962, 1964, 1965, 1987 by The Lockman Foundation. Used by permission.

Scripture quotations labeled KJV are from the King James Version of the Bible.

Scripture quotations labeled NASB are from the New American Standard Bible®, copyright © 1960, 1962, 1963, 1968, 1971, 1972, 1973, 1975, 1977, 1995 by The Lockman Foundation. Used by permission.

Scripture quotations labeled NIV are from the Holy Bible, New International Version®. NIV®. Copyright © 1973, 1978, 1984 by Biblica, Inc.™ Used by permission of Zondervan. All rights reserved worldwide. www.zondervan.com

Scripture quotations labeled NKJV are from the New King James Version. Copyright © 1982 by Thomas Nelson, Inc. Used by permission. All rights reserved.

Scripture quotations labeled TLB are from The Living Bible, copyright © 1971. Used by permission of Tyndale House Publishers, Inc., Wheaton, Illinois 60189. All rights reserved.

Cover design by David Griffing
Edited by Kathy Deering and Rose Decaen

CONTENTS

FOREWORD

Anger and women—we've all been confused about how to handle this volatile emotion. We've been told to stuff it or strut it, but in truth, neither of these behaviors will get us what we ultimately want. And even when there are reasons to get angry, we women don't really want to fight, we want to win! Far too often, though, the "victory" results in losing at both love and life; friends become strangers and children and loved ones get pushed away. Our health becomes compromised and we find our emotions spiraling downward. Compassionate understanding of this emotion called anger has never been so desperately needed!

Women who hang on to unresolved anger issues either end up pushing away the very ones they long to draw near or they turn the anger on themselves. I know, because I've done both.

When I was a stay-at-home mom with three boys under age five, I had the privilege of reading my first book by these caring men, Norm Wright and Gary Oliver. At that time I wanted so desperately to gather all the information I could to "do it right" and pass a blessing on to my children. But instead I ended each day exhausted and with a list in my head of how I had failed to do just that. I remember one night when I climbed in bed with the book, hoping to draw on its wisdom, and came across the question of what our goal, as parents, should be for our children. My mind raced to fill in the blank. *I am going to get this answer correct!* I thought to myself. I wrote out an impressive résumé of attributes and felt very self-satisfied as I turned the page to check my answer. What I read shook every paradigm I held as a mother. It was so simple yet profound that it still remains with me today, as a mother of four—three of whom are teens. The gist of the answer is that our goal as parents should be to cause our children to be independent from us and dependent on God. I immediately felt released and empowered.

I believe you will also feel released and empowered when you read *A Woman's Forbidden Emotion*. It is time to heal the hurts of women young and old. For mothers who are confused and trapped in their past, and

for their daughters who often relive their mothers' wounds, it is time to
time to experience God's love and forgiveness and to let Him wash away
all the hurt of yesterday. It is time to become equipped with the skills we
need to move beyond shame and condemnation to a position of repen-
tance and empowerment. It is my prayer that destructive anger would no
longer be passed from one generation to another, as though it were an
inheritance. It is time to pass something more to our sons and our
daughters.

So be encouraged. The Father has come with healing in His wings.
This book is filled with tender and insightful instruction that fosters a
safe environment for the Holy Spirit to shed His light of truth on your
heart and life. It will guide you to the root of the issue so that you will
not spend the rest of your life pulling off the fruit.

Lisa Bevere
Speaker and author
Be Angry But Don't Blow It! and *Kissed the Girls and Made Them Cry*

PREFACE

This is a book that almost didn't get written. We (Norm and Gary) have been friends for more than 30 years, and some of our favorite and most productive times together have been on a variety of fishing trips. When the fish didn't bite, we would often discuss what God was doing in our own lives, in our marriages and families—and in the lives of those who were coming to us for counseling.

After many discussions, we became aware of the need for a book that would help women understand the biblical teaching on anger, and the role of healthy anger in both individual and relational health. At that time the majority of people who came to us for counseling were women—and many of these good women were struggling with an emotion they had been told they weren't supposed to have. It was okay for their husbands and other men in their lives to have it. It was okay for their kids to have it. But it wasn't okay for good Christian women to have it. Of course, the "it" I'm referring to is the emotion of anger.

By God's grace we were able to help many of these women understand anger from a biblical perspective. We taught them how to experience and express it in ways that were consistent with Scripture, which increased their effectiveness in their relationships and significantly decreased the many unhealthy effects that result when anger is dealt with inappropriately.

On numerous occasions we talked about writing a book that addressed the issue of women and anger. The only problem was that we were two men. We thought it might be at best presumptuous and at worst sexist and arrogant for two men to write such a book.

However, in our seminars and workshops and in our counseling interactions (at that time the majority of those we counseled were women), we were encouraged by those same women to write this book. As we surveyed more than 3,000 women of all ages from across the country—as well as nationally known leaders of women's ministries—in an effort to learn more about women and anger, we continued to be encouraged to write about anger and women. We're glad we finally listened to these women (sometimes it takes men a while to get it)! And while many books go out of print in their first year of publication, this book has been in print for close to 10 years. Now we're delighted that it is coming out in a fresh, revised edition for a new generation of women.

One of our greatest surprises from *Good Women Get Angry* (original title for *A Woman's Forbidden Emotion*) has been the number of men—that's right, men—who told us that this book was one of the most helpful resources they had ever read. Because of our book, these men were able to better understand their wives and daughters and to interact more effectively with them. When we wrote this book originally, we didn't have men in mind. After hearing so much positive feedback from men (primarily from men we met at Promise Keepers events), we went back through the book with a "new set of eyes" and saw how it actually could be valuable for men to read. So, if you are a man who is reading this and wondering if it will help you understand the woman in your life, the answer is yes!

Another surprise for us was the number of moms who read the book and then bought a copy for their daughters. Numerous women either wrote or told us that taking their daughters through the book gave them an opportunity to teach an awareness of anger as well as specific skills and resources they desperately wished they'd had when they were teenagers. Several moms said that because it was a book they were both *reading*, they were able to teach their daughters about anger more effectively than if they had merely tried to tell their daughters the same information. During the teenaged years, telling sons or daughters anything tends not to be the most effective form of communication. So if you're a mom looking for a way to connect with your daughter, this book might prove to be a great first step.

One final observation: Our book has helped many believers understand that there is a difference between healthy and unhealthy anger, that all anger isn't bad, that anger is a God-given emotion, that anger is discussed frequently in the Bible, and that healthy anger can actually increase our effectiveness in life and in our relationships. We hope that the positive and redemptive aspects of this powerful emotion (the second most frequently mentioned emotion in the Bible) encourage all those who read this revised edition. And we hope that anger will no longer be the forbidden emotion in the life of any woman!

ACKNOWLEDGMENTS

We owe a debt of gratitude to the many women (and a few men) across the country who contributed to the research for this book.

Much of our information regarding the kinds of pressures women face and how they deal with them came from more than 3,000 surveys of women across the United States. Those who helped us collect those surveys include Virgil and Evelyn Ediger, Steve and Twyla Lee, Paul and Kathy Nauman, and Jolene Kelley.

Early in our research process we sent more extensive surveys to a variety of women who have been involved in ministry to women on a denominational or national level—or both. All of these women, though busy, were kind enough to take the time to respond to our questions. Their insights, concerns and questions were very helpful. Their gracious participation in our research does not imply their endorsement of what we have written:

Elisabeth Elliot	Karen Mains
Ruby Friesen	Carol Mayhall
Diana Garland	Lee McDowell
Pamela Heim	Shirley Stevens
Kay Lindskoog	Sandra Wilson

Additional thanks go to Carrie Oliver, Lanell Schilling, Carol Golz, Lynn Trathen, Naomi Gaede Penner and Marilyn McGinnis for helpful discussions and contributions. Thanks go as well to Judy Coddington and Kristi Buhler for typing the manuscript; to Bryn Edwards for the efficient orchestrating of a multitude of details in the office.

A special word of thanks to Maryellen Stipe, who gave many hours to helping in literature reviews and tracking down hard-to-find articles in journals and magazines—and remained joyous throughout the process. In addition to her contribution to our research, her group of more than 200 women at the Crossroads Church in Denver provided invaluable feedback to us regarding some of the ideas presented in this book.

CHAPTER 1

ANGER—FRIEND OR FOE?

H. Norman Wright

We asked more than 2,400 women to respond to a survey. Here are some of the most typical answers to the part of the survey that involved completing the sentence,

When I get angry, I . . .

- usually keep my anger inside and let it build up until I'm basically fed up.
- don't immediately express it. I rationalize the situation, or I contemplate the cause and validity of my reaction to the cause.
- get sarcastic and biting in my comments. I fish for someone to ask me what is wrong.
- find it easy to stuff it and get depressed.
- fume inside and snap at people. I do use words to express it, but I become snappy and impatient.
- drive myself crazy.
- get ugly. If I happen to walk by a mirror, I am surprised at how hateful I look. I want to hurt back with words. I want

that person to be sorry they hurt me, and then I am sorry at
my own selfishness.

- am probably more negative. I tend to clam up, and I know that
is wrong.
- scream.
- yell, then cry.
- feel sad for feeling that way—then I lose my patience.
- feel out of control and lash out—I regret my behavior later. I
even hate myself at the time, but I can't seem to stop.
- either button up for a while, or I rage like a crazy person; or I
express myself passionately but in a controlled way.
- hit a wall, throw something, yell, say something I regret, slam a
door.
- tend to yell and want to hit someone.
- tend to draw inward with my emotions and then feel very guilty.
- Sometimes walk away and let it simmer underneath. Sometimes
I raise my voice and express it. Sometimes I yell. Sometimes I
take the person aside and talk calmly about it.

Anger—is a strange and puzzling feeling, isn't it? It's not a signal to
be ignored, like a postcard sent at a bulk rate. It's more like a special
delivery letter telling you that you're being hurt, your rights are being
trampled, you're living in fear, you're frustrated or you're ignoring something significant in your life. You could be feeling anger because you're
trying too hard to please others and are neglecting yourself; or maybe
you're being doted on too much by others and feeling deprived of the
chance to grow and become more independent.

Were you ever taught how to understand anger as you were growing
up? Did your mother or father sit down with you and say, "Let me tell
you about anger"?

Who Taught You How to Become Angry?

In our survey, we asked the question, Who taught you how to become
angry? Here are some of the responses:

- Both parents. My father was slow to anger, but more to be feared when provoked. For my mother, it was a daily, frequent ritual of outbursts.
- Born a sinner—don't think I needed to be taught.
- Myself, from watching my sister and mother, and sometimes my dad, because he would stuff his feelings (for years) until one day he would explode.
- My family taught me how *not* to become angry, and I hope God's Word and His Holy Spirit taught and are teaching me how to become angry.
- I think there was lots of anger stuffed in marriage, a hard marriage. Husband gone all the time and left me with full responsibility. Lots of anger came from him—men in general.
- Some book about two kinds of anger—righteous and unrighteous (after I was an adult).
- No one taught me how to become angry. I think anger is a natural human emotion.

Did anyone teach you that it's all right to be angry because this can help you improve relationships and correct wrongs in your life? This was probably not the message you heard when you were growing up. If you are like many women, you probably heard, "Don't rock the boat. Be a peacemaker. Your job is to nurture others. And don't show a man your anger. It will drive him away." Studies show that this message is widespread in our culture. "Anger in men is often viewed as 'masculine'—it is seen as 'manly' when men engage in fistfights or act their anger out physically. But for girls, acting out is not encouraged. Women usually get the message that anger is unpleasant and unfeminine."[1]

There have been so many restrictions against women feeling and expressing anger that it is difficult for many women even to know they are angry. I've heard the phrase "she's just irrational" used many times when a woman was expressing her anger, as though a label could explain it away. Over the past decades, when women became angry they were looked on as unfeminine and were usually described in uncomplimentary language. Women are called "witches," "nags" or "man-haters," to name just a few.

"These are words for an angry woman: bitch, shrew, nag. . . . Deborah
Cox quotes one conversation in *Women's Anger*, a book she co-authored,
'a researcher asks a group of girls: "What do you look like when you're
angry?" "Ugly," the girls reply.'"[2]

Traditionally, women have expressed their anger in indirect ways.
Those could take the form of acting hurt, being wounded or sulking—all
of which fit the image of being "nice." But being a placater and overrid-
ing one's true feelings, hopes, desires and dreams lead to an accumulation of anger. I've talked to a number of women in counseling over the
years who have had this experience. They say, "I really don't do too well
getting angry, but I'm quite adept at feeling guilty. At least then I'm the
only one that gets hurt." But that isn't really true either, for that guilt
leads to anger—and one way or another, anger is going to find an outlet,
whether one wants it to or not.

At Home and at Work

The anger is there for a number of reasons. It could be caused by a
woman's feeling that she must live up to male expectations that she be
fragile, dependent, helpless and willing to follow a man's dictates.[3] It
may be caused by her not being taken seriously in meetings when she
voices her opinion, or by her being asked to take notes or get the coffee
in the meeting because she is a woman. It could be caused by her having
to put up with male behavior that is rude and rejecting toward women
in general. I have also observed similar behavior many times in phone
conversations and even at my office; a man will be rude to one of my sec-
retaries, whereas he wouldn't think of talking to me in the same manner.
On occasions when I confront a caller about this issue, his attitude
toward my secretary the next time he calls is amazingly different. The
discrepancy in the way men and women are treated can also be seen
when a man voices a complaint and gets more response to it than a
woman would if she were to make the same complaint.

The labels men apply to women are another source of anger. "She's
just hysterical; she'll calm down," a man might say. Another put-down:
"Here comes the PMS again. It's time to avoid her for a few days."

Many women feel powerless to do much about their situation. They engage in blame, and whenever blame is alive it leads to anger. Fear is another major cause of anger; consequently, as our society becomes increasingly unsafe for women, we see their anger on the increase. I have a friend whose daughter was almost raped. My wife and grown daughter both carry a protective spray whenever they are out, and there are certain places my wife will not go in the evening. I have worked with assault victims and have seen the fear and rage they experience over what has happened to them.

We see more anger at home and at work. Within the home much of the anger stems from the division of the workload. Women who work outside the home must spend many additional hours in housework each week compared to men, and both men and women are angry at the lack of appreciation they receive from their partner.[4] At work, women continue to be frustrated by the fact that, in certain professions, they earn less than their male counterparts. (Fortunately, however, there are a number of professions in which one's gender does not matter).

But it is not just these various forms of social injustice that are causing women to respond in anger. In our national survey, we asked women: What are some of the factors which increase your vulnerability to anger? The respondents were given four spaces in which to list their answers (not in order of importance).

In a sampling of 722 surveys in which this question was answered, we discovered the following:

- 48 percent identified fatigue or being tired.
- 28 percent mentioned stress.
- 20 percent said injustice.
- 14 percent mentioned children.
- 13 percent said PMS.
- 11 percent said pain or illness.
- 9 percent stated feeling out of control or helplessness.
- 8 percent identified frustration.
- 7 percent said communication with their husbands.
- 7 percent said it was a spiritual problem.

Passive-Aggressive Expression of Anger

Despite the fact that it is becoming more socially acceptable for women to express their feelings, many women still go underground with their anger. One particularly unhealthy approach is to express anger by being passive-aggressive—being angry but expressing it in a disguised way. Some people are clever at this. They may or may not be conscious that they are angry, but whatever their level of awareness, they convey their anger unmistakably—and indirectly. They may release it under the guise of critical comments, or they may harbor well-camouflaged resentment. If confronted, they proclaim their innocence. Their response is similar to the description in Proverbs 26:18-19: "As a madman who casts firebrands, arrows and death, so is the man who deceives his neighbor and then says, Was I not joking?" (*AMP*).

> *Despite the fact that it is becoming more socially acceptable for women to express their feelings, many women still go underground with their anger.*

What particular responses might you adopt if you're a passive-aggressive?

Letting out your anger by procrastinating is one tactic.[5] Putting off responsibilities or delaying doing something for someone else is another disguised way to vent your anger. It's not obvious and so it feels safe because it's difficult for others to label the action as anger. You're more comfortable being called "irresponsible" or "lazy" than be labeled "angry."

Subtle stubbornness is another expression of anger. So is forgetting or avoidance. These behaviors usually reflect anger that you wouldn't dare express openly.

Forgetting is another handy way to express anger, because the responsibility can be turned back against the other person. "Are you *sure* you asked me?" Or, "Are you *sure* that was the time we agreed upon?"

"I'm so sorry you had to wait in the rain. But I was *sure* you said to pick you up at 10:30 and not at 10. Well, anyway, you can get some dry clothes at home." When passive-aggressives say things like this, others begin to doubt themselves. They end up feeling responsible. But the truth is they have been set up.

How else might you express anger indirectly? Using your spouse's car and leaving it a mess, and with an empty gas tank, works well. Paying a bill but conveniently forgetting to mail it can bring your spouse an unpleasant call from the gas company. You can take the money out of your partner's wallet and fail to let him know about it. You can be passive-aggressive by walking over to the TV as someone is viewing his favorite program and turning the channel to something you want to watch.

Sarcasm is another "nice" way to be angry. Two messages are given at one time, a compliment and a put-down. "You look so young I didn't recognize you." "Your new suit is radical, but I like it."

I've seen passive-aggressives act as though they didn't understand the simplest instructions. Though there might be a slight smile or give-away smirk on their faces, confronting them usually doesn't work. They play innocent; and if you ever suggest that they might be angry, you're likely to get a "Who me? I'm not angry at all!" response. You'll end up wondering if you're the one with the problem.

Many women think, *If I become angry, won't I become aggressive too?* I don't think so. For many years we connected anger and aggression. But there is actually not as much connection between anger and aggression as there is between anger and blame. We don't tend to become as angry when we understand the what and why of another person's response. That is especially important in significant relationships. When you lack an object of blame, do you become angry? Not usually.

Anger as a Protector and a Defense

Another often-overlooked characteristic of anger could be operating in your life at this time. Anger acts as a protector and a defense. When the hormonal changes of anger kicks in, you will find that you can defend yourself better. Why?

Your anger gives you a feeling of empowerment. The doubts that you had about yourself are disappearing. You now have sufficient energy to cope. Your anger is a newfound source of strength to mobilize yourself.

Your anger helps you to block out fear and guilt. Anger tends to drive away any feeling that might inhibit you. Unless you turn your anger back against yourself, it will push you ahead to attack.

Your anger helps you to focus on your own needs rather than the other person's. Your pain and needs are the focus, not the other person's. You are convinced that you are right, and your anger strengthens this belief. (This is why some men and women become addicted to anger, for at no other time do they have these feelings.)

Perhaps the best way to illustrate how we use our anger as a defense is by giving examples.

- *We use anger to alleviate the pain of guilt.* Are you familiar with guilt? If so, you know how uncomfortable it is. To alleviate the pain of guilt and defend ourselves against it, we can become angry against what another person is making us feel guilty about. This works for a while but doesn't resolve the problem.
- *We use anger to defend against hurt.* That hurt might stem from an unkind remark, a rejection or an injustice. In lashing out we cover the pain of hurt.
- *We use anger to defend against a loss.* I've seen people react with anger when a son or daughter goes off to college or to work in another part of the country, or when a friend moves away. Anger often arises when we lose a loved one in death. We find something to blame in the person and focus on the hurt we are experiencing instead of on the delight he or she may be experiencing.
- *We use anger as a defense against the feeling of being trapped or helpless.* You may be working overtime to pay for your children's braces. You didn't realize how long it would take or how expensive it would be, and now you're stuck on a treadmill for the next two years. You don't have any alternative but to stick it out, so you begin to think, *They don't even appreciate what they're getting,* and you focus on your exhaustion and lack of time for yourself. So

it's no wonder that quarrels between you and your children have increased as you find more and more to become angry about. They see you as being overly critical, which you may be, but it's your outlet against being trapped.

• *We use anger as a defense against fear.* You've probably seen this in others or have experienced it yourself. A child runs into the street, and fear propels the mother into the street to grab her child in front of a car. She yells and spanks the child in anger, which covers her feelings of fear.

Using anger to defend against painful feelings is normal. The problem arises when we make anger a habit, or when the frequency and intensity of our anger begin to affect us and our relationships.

Anger can become an addiction. Anger addicts have used anger as a defense for so long that they know no other way to respond; they feel empty without the rush of anger. That is the down side of anger. People who use anger as a defense over a period of time have a hard time letting go of it—especially if they find it easier to feel anger than to feel fear, hurt, guilt or emptiness.

All addictions feel good for the moment, but they don't help us to resolve the problems we face. A response of anger may be appropriate and helpful in situations where we face a direct threat. But the habitual, addictive type of anger will probably direct us a way from whatever appropriate action would help resolve the problem.

What Anger Keeps Us from Accomplishing

If anger has the capacity to help block out painful feelings, why should we deal with the original pain and its cause? We should do so because confronting the original pain and its cause is essential if we are to become whole.

Anger Keeps Us from Confronting the Source of Our Fear

Anger will keep you from distinguishing between actual threats and distortions that create fear. It will keep you from confronting negative messages you say to yourself—things that you may have learned from poor experiences with your parents or other significant individuals in your life. You may be using anger to silence and override this self-critical voice that goes of inside your head from time to time. But will anger help you confront that critic and evict it from your life? Not usually.

Anger Keeps Guilt Alive

When you use anger as a defense, you will never come to the place where you deal with the source of your guilt. Your guilt may arise from false beliefs, or it may result from your giving priority to fulfilling your needs rather than living by your value system. You become angry at yourself when you know you are violating your values, but that doesn't stop you from doing it again and again.

> *All of this is not to say that you should never become angry. Quite the contrary. It's when anger becomes your main line of defense that it becomes a difficulty.*

Anger Keeps Grief Alive

Many times I have seen grief kept alive by anger over a major loss in someone's life. Anger can keep a person from saying good-bye to whatever has been lost. It can push them to keep reliving the hurts, harsh words and wrongs of the relationship—which just reinforces the pain, guilt and intensity of the loss.

Anger Closes Off Communication

I've rarely met an angry person who is able to talk about what pains him or her when angry. Yet if you are unable to talk about what is hurting you when you are angry, how can other people know what is bothering you? How can they change their response to you if you don't let them know how you felt wounded by what they said or did?

Anger Keeps Us Feeling Like Victims

You feel helpless in spite of the strength of your anger because your anger doesn't let you fix what's wrong. When you blame or defend, your energy is diverted from resolving the original problem.

All of this is not to say that you should never become angry. Quite the contrary. It's when anger becomes your main line of defense that it becomes a difficulty. Every concern and issue has a solution, but anger doesn't usually lead you to that solution.[6]

Silent Pain

Anger within a woman that goes unrecognized, unadmitted and untouched becomes an unwanted resident that soon affects the totality of her life. *Silent Pain*, the title of a 1992 book for women, refers to the submerged sadness or deep ache that results and that is always there just underneath the surface, taking the edge off life. That pain could reflect deep unfulfilled longings, disappointments in relationships or lingering unhealed hurts.[7]

There are many reasons for silent pain. It could be a residual grief from the past that has never been resolved. Years ago I learned to ask my counselees the question, What is there in your life that you've never fully grieved over? In time most identify some loss—and with each loss there is usually a residue of anger.

It could be pain over a current situation that reminds you of a similar past heartache, but you don't feel free to talk about it. You're angry that it still exists, but you can't talk about the anger either.

It could be connected to a sense of shame over a past or present sin, real or imagined. You believe that what you did was so wrong you cannot be forgiven, so you live with your pain. Underneath may be a residual anger over the unfairness of the continuation of that pain.

When you bury any emotion, there is a loss. When you bury your sorrow and don't allow yourself to feel your sadness, you don't realize your need for comfort and consolation. When you bury your anger, you ignore what it's trying to tell you. In so doing you may create another nemesis more common to women than to men—depression.

Some women take a long time to feel angry after an unpleasant event has occurred. But the fuel for the anger is there. The ingredients, the shape, the structure and the energy are all there, whether ignored or not. What happens to all that energy? Where does it go?

Anger and Depression

In many cases that anger results in depression.

Why is it that women experience depression more than men? Why is it that one in every four women will suffer a serious clinical depression at some time in her life, whereas only one in eight men will? According to a 1990 study by the American Psychological Association, it is not because women are more willing to share their feelings, to complain or go for counseling. It is instead because women have not been culturally conditioned to combat depression.[8] A chain reaction toward depression is involved. Women's vulnerability to depression may be connected to their tendency toward passivity and dependency, which they confuse with being feminine. This leads to a hesitation to admit, face and resolve their anger. Men are given permission by society to be angry, whereas women are not, which in turn leads many women to feel it necessary to suppress their anger. Since anger that is suppressed does not just go away, suppressing anger makes women more prone to anger. That in turn leads to depression, for suppressed anger is often channeled into depression.[9] In a later chapter depression will be dealt with in detail.

Unfortunately, many women learn this pattern as young children. Growing up in a dysfunctional family retards emotional expression, whether the dysfunction is divorce, alcoholism, abuse or perfectionism. What happens between a woman and her father is a key factor. Any type of abandonment is damaging, whether it be by emotional withdrawal, death or divorce.

This learned repression of emotions is what keeps a woman stuck in her pain. Some believe that emotional distress is caused not so much by the painful events of life, but by silence about those events and the feelings underneath them. I've seen this tragedy in the counseling office with women in their 30s and 40s, who for the first time in their lives are taking the cap off their repressed emotions and beginning to face them. It is interesting to see the transformation that occurs. As they let their feelings out, especially anger, they discover a newfound source of energy.

Positive Ways of Dealing with Anger

What can you do about anger? First of all, accept it. Break out of the repressive mode. Anger has a message for you. It's there for a reason.

So discover the reason for your anger. What is the real cause in each situation? As you look at each situation or encounter in which you are angry, ask yourself, "What is bothering me, and what would I like to change?" Then ask, "What can I do to change?"

You may find that sometimes your anger response is different with different individuals. You may argue with one individual, yell at another, use silent withdrawal from another, push intensely toward another and distance yourself physically and emotionally from someone else. Which do you do with whom, and why? Who sees you as angry? Who never sees your anger? Which persons do you want to know about your anger?

You can learn the difference between expressing your anger aggressively and expressing it assertively. You can learn when you are using anger to defend and when you are using it to blame. Once you are able to express your anger without yelling, blaming or attacking, you will feel better about what you are saying, and others will hear you more clearly. Later in this book you will learn the steps involved in the process.

When you express your hurt in honest ways, other people will be freed to be just as honest with you. Then growth in your relationships can occur.

When you express your hurt and disappointment in honest, controlled and constructive ways, other people will be freed to be just as honest with you. Then growth in your relationships can occur. Relationships can survive and even improve when disagreements are handled properly. When you express anger properly, it will have the effect of exposing you to the criticism and challenges of others. It will force you to stop blaming other people and consider your own responsibilities for a change. If you suppress anger or explode, it won't provide the advantage of constructive expression that opens you up to an evaluation of your own behavior. Suppression and constant defensive anger are ineffective ways of dealing with anger.

Don't apologize for your anger. If it's there, accept it. It's yours. Use it for change. As a woman, you need not be uncomfortable with the anger you feel. Instead, see it as a messenger telling you about the cause. Then, with God's love and help, tackle the cause.

Take Action

Here is a survey on anger beliefs that well over 1,000 women completed. Before going on to the next chapter, please take a few minutes and complete it for yourself. You'll find it helpful in applying the rest of the information in this book.

Anger Beliefs

Please read through the following list of anger beliefs.

If, at any time in your life, you have either outwardly agreed to a particular belief or, by your actions, have functioned according to it, circle the number that most accurately expresses the degree of your agreement with that belief.

1 = Strongly Agree
2 = Moderately Agree
3 = Neutral
4 = Moderately Disagree
5 = Strongly Disagree

1. God is love and anger is the opposite of love. Therefore, God is against anger. Whenever we allow ourselves to be angry, we are sinning.

   1   2   3   4   5

2. If a person never looks or sounds angry, she doesn't have a problem with anger.

   1   2   3   4   5

3. Anger always leads to some form of violence and, therefore, it is never good to be angry.

   1   2   3   4   5

4. If you express anger to someone you love, it will destroy the relationship. Anger and love don't mix.

   1   2   3   4   5

5. The best way to deal with anger is to ignore it. If you ignore it, it will go away.

   1   2   3   4   5

6. The best way to deal with anger is to snuff it. Expressing anger breeds even more anger and leads to loss of control.

   1   2   3   4   5

7. The best way to deal with anger is to dump it, just get all of that anger out of your system. You and everyone else will feel better when you express it.

   1   2   3   4   5

8. Nice people don't get angry.

   1   2   3   4   5

Please answer the following questions true or false.

9. It is more acceptable for men to express anger than women.
   T F

10. I often feel guilty about my anger. T F

11. I don't know how to express my anger appropriately. T F

12. I wish I weren't such an angry person. T F

13. I'm afraid that if I get in touch with my anger I will lose control.
   T F

14. It's hard for me to know when I'm angry. T F

Please respond to the following questions and statements.

15. What are some of the factors that increase your vulnerability to anger?
    a.
    b.
    c.
    d.
16. When you hear the word "anger," do you tend to have a positive or negative response to that word?
    Positive   Negative
17. From your point of view, is anger primarily a positive or a negative emotion?
    Positive   Negative
18. When I get angry I . . .
19. When someone around me gets angry, I . . .
20. When I was a child, the primary *times* in which I saw anger expressed were . . .
21. The *ways* in which I saw anger expressed were . . .
22. Who taught you how to *become* angry?
23. Who taught you how to *express* anger?
24. If there is any one question that I could have answered about anger it would be . . .

CHAPTER 2

WHAT IS ANGER?

Gary J. Oliver

In the sticky spring air of that Texas night, the smell of honeysuckle hung in the air. The howling of mating cats woke Lowell from his tormented sleep. Years ago his back had been broken in a fall from a Santa Fe Railroad water tank car that had jerked into action before he could get down the ladder. He had fallen on a pile of rock and crushed his back, costing him nine months in a body cast. That old injury prevented him from getting a good night's rest, but this night was noisy too, and that meant trouble.

Lowell rose from his hard bed, cursed the cats under his breath, then went straight to the closet where he kept his .22 rifle. Since the house was in the country almost at the end of the road, there was a lot of open space and no ordinances. Lowell walked out into the backyard, listened for telling sounds and fired into the darkness. A screech, the silence, as the bullet found its mark. In silence he returned the gun to the closet and himself to the bed for a few more hours of fitful sleep until dawn broke.

At dawn Lowell pulled on his shirt and faded blue denim overalls, pushed his flat feet into the old brogues he wore daily. Outside, the dew hung heavy on the vines, grass and flowers. On the edge of the garden near the rows of foot-high corn lay the cat, still and quiet. Its gray form was stiff from rigor mortis, its fur matted with dirt and thick red blood that oozed from the fatal wound. Lowell picked her up by the tail and walked toward the carport, intending to throw the cat in his truck and haul her away.

Ruth was up early cooking breakfast and the smells distracted Lowell from his task. He dropped the cat along the edge of the flower bed and came inside for bacon, eggs, biscuits and gravy. Forgotten were the events of the night before when Lowell left for work. With her husband fed and gone, Ruth washed the dishes and got ready for another hot day of housework.

Their daughter, Laura, awoke, trying to remember if what happened last night was real or a dream. When she heard the closet door open last night while the cats fought in the yard, Laura did what she had done so many times before to "disappear." She pulled the pillow over her head and stuck her fingers in her ears, hoping not to hear the gun go off. How she hated that sound. This morning she was not sure if it had really happened.

In her usual routine, Laura arose to inspect the flowers and garden to see what miracles had appeared overnight. The hollyhocks were open wide—pink, white, red and rose colored with big-bodied black and yellow bumblebees already at work inside them gathering nectar. There were giant golden squash blossoms on the sprawling green vines and tiny white bean flowers. As Laura ran to the flower bed, she spotted Patty's gray fur, the blood almost dried. Stunned, she stopped, caught her breath, then wheeled around and ran in the house crying.

By the time she reached the back screen door Ruth heard her sobs. She thought Laura must have been stung by a bee as she investigated a flower too closely. If only that were all it was! Laura ran to her mother sobbing and screaming, "Why does he do that? Can't he stop shooting long enough to see?" Why had her dad shot her cat, not the stray tom that had come courting?

There were no answers then, or ever. Obviously, Lowell had forgotten the cat after breakfast, leaving it to be found by his heartbroken, terrified child. Laura never knew what he would find as a target next. One day her cat, the next a rabbit. When would it be her turn? Somewhere deep inside she knew her dad would like to turn her into a target also. She felt marked for death as surely as if she wore a red circle on her forehead.[1]

This is a true story. Laura grew up learning that anger was harmful, dangerous, destructive and something to avoid. And she tried hard to avoid it. For most of her life she repressed, suppressed, stuffed, denied and ignored anything that even came close to anger. After all, she had learned well the effects of anger by watching her father Lowell. She knew that nothing good ever came from being angry.

As she got older it became harder and harder for her to deny and stuff her anger. She didn't want it, she didn't understand it, she didn't know what to do with it, but it was there. She was concerned about her spirituality because she had been raised with the misbelief that "nice Christian girls don't get angry." She had also learned the "no talk" rule. Whatever went on at home should never be talked about to anyone outside of the home. Thus any kind of counseling was out of the question.

Over time she realized that her struggle with the emotion she didn't understand but could no longer deny was affecting almost every area of her life. The walls she had built and the emotional medication of busyness and denial that had for a time been helpful were no longer effective. God used a crisis to lead Laura to move beyond her fear and reach out for help.

Anger Defined

What is anger? Anger is one of the most complex and multidimensional emotions; it is thus one of the most difficult to define.

When I have asked groups of people to define "anger," I have received almost as many different definitions of anger as there were people in the audience. A. D. Lester, in his book *The Angry Christian*, defines anger as "the physical, mental, and emotional arousal pattern that occurs in response to a perceived threat to the self, characterized by the desire to attack or defend."[2]

The English word "anger" is derived from an old Norse word *angre*, which means "affliction." In German, *Arger* is the noun of *arg*, which means "wicked"; thus *Arger* is the emotional response to "wicked" stimuli.

In Spanish, *enojar* (to get angry) derives from *en* and *ojo*—"something that offends the eye." In these languages, anger refers to uneasiness, displeasure and resentment.

Another valuable way of understanding anger is to look at what God's Word has to say about it. As I began to study the emotion of anger, I started by looking in the Bible. I was surprised to find that the Word of God has a lot to say about anger and uses a number of different words to describe the various types of anger. The first mention of anger occurs in Genesis 4:5, the last reference to anger is found in Revelation 19:15. In the Old Testament alone anger is mentioned 455 times with 375 of those references dealing with God's anger.

In the Old Testament, the word for anger actually meant "nostril" or "nose." In ancient Hebrew psychology, the nose was thought to be the seat of anger. The phrase "slow to anger" literally means "long of nose." Sometimes people's nostrils can flare as the intensity of their feelings causes physiological changes.

Numerous synonyms for anger used in the Old Testament. They include ill-humor and rage (see Esther 1:12), overflowing rage and fury (see Amos 1:11), and indignation (see Jer. 15:17). Anger is implied in the Old Testament through words such as "revenge," "cursing," "jealousy," "snorting" and "grinding the teeth."

Several words are used for anger in the New Testament. It is critical to understand the distinction between these words. I've had many people remark that the Scripture appears to contradict itself because in one verse we are taught not to be angry and in another we are admonished to "be angry and sin not." Which is the correct interpretation and which should we follow?

The most common New Testament word for anger is "orge." It is used 45 times and means a more settled and long-lasting attitude of anger that is slower in its onset but more enduring. This kind of anger is similar to coals on a barbecue slowly warming up to red and then white hot and holding that temperature until the cooking is done. But it often includes revenge.

In two places in the New Testament where the term "anger" is used, revenge is not included in the meaning. In Ephesians 4:26 we are taught "Be angry, and yet do not sin; do not let the sun go down on your anger" (*NASB*). In the Greek, the term used for "anger" in the first part of this verse (*orge*) is different from the anger in the second half (*parorgismos*) where we are told not to let the sun go down upon our anger.

In Mark 3:5, Jesus looks upon the Pharisees "with anger." In this passage and in Ephesians 4:26, the word "anger" refers to an abiding habit of the mind that is aroused under certain conditions against evil and injustice. This is the type of anger that Christians are encouraged to have—an anger that does not include revenge or rage.

Another frequently used Greek term for anger in the New Testament is "thumas." "Thumas" is anger as a turbulent commotion or a boiling agitation of feelings. This type of anger blazes up into a sudden explosion whereas in "orge" there is an occasional element of deliberate thought. "Thumas" is an outburst from inner indignation and is similar to a match that quickly ignites into a blaze but then burns out rapidly. This type of anger is mentioned 18 times (see, for example, Eph. 4:31 and Gal. 5:20). This is the type of anger we are called upon to control.

A type of anger mentioned only three times in the New Testament, and never in a positive sense, is *parorgismos*. "Parorgismos" is a stronger form of "orge" and refers to anger that has been provoked. It is characterized by irritation, exasperation or embitterment. "Do not ever let your wrath—your exasperation, your fury or indignation—last until the sun goes down" (Eph. 4:26, *AMP*).

> *From the nursery to the nursing home, the emotion of anger is a universal experience.*

Important Characteristics of Anger

What do we need to know about anger to help it work for us rather than against us?

Anger Is a God-Given Emotion

No human being—nobody, male or female—is immune from experiencing the full range of human emotions. God created us this way. One of the occupational hazards of being human is that we experience emotions, *all* the emotions, including the basic human emotion of anger. From the nursery to the nursing home, the emotion of anger is a universal experience.

Anger Is a Secondary Emotion

Anger is an almost automatic response to any kind of pain. It is the emotion that most people feel shortly after they have been hurt. When you trip and fall or stub your toe it hurts and you may experience mild anger. When your spouse forgets a birthday or anniversary, it hurts. When a good friend says she will meet you for lunch and then doesn't show up, it hurts, and you may experience anger. When your teenaged son or daughter is out two hours past his or her 11:00 P.M. curfew and hasn't called, you may experience concern and fear. When he or she waltzes in the door and calmly announces, "Sorry, Mom, I forgot to call," you may experience anger.

Anger Is Often the First Emotion That We See

Sometimes it's the only emotion that we are aware of. However, it is rarely the only one we have experienced. Just below the surface are almost always other emotions that need to be identified and acknowledged. Hidden deep underneath surface anger are fear, hurt, frustration, disappointment, vulnerability and longing for connection.

At a very early age, many of us learned that anger can help us divert attention from these more painful emotions. Anger is safer. It provides a sense of protection for the frightened and vulnerable self. It can provide a temporary sense of distance from our seeming helplessness. It doesn't take long to learn that it's easier to feel anger than it is to feel pain. Anger provides an increase of energy. It can decrease our sense of vulnerability and thus increase our sense of security. It is often a false security, but it is a kind of security nonetheless.

Anger Is a Powerful Emotion

In our experience, when most people think about anger they associate it with the most painful and violent expression of anger they have seen or heard. Anger is often associated with (and confused with) hostility, rage, aggression, violence and destruction. And it is true that when anger gets out of control it can be expressed in horrible ways. But the problem isn't the anger. The problem is the people haven't learned how to understand and value their anger, how to listen to their anger, how to hear the warnings their anger provides.

Anger Involves Power

When you are angry you feel "charged up" and ready for action. Physiologically, anger triggers an outpouring of adrenaline and other stress hormones to your central and peripheral nervous systems, with noticeable physical consequences. Your voice changes to a higher pitch. The rate and depth of your breathing increases. Your perspiration increases. Your heart beats faster and harder. The muscles of your arms and legs may tighten up. The digestive process slows down. You may feel as though a war is being waged in your head and stomach.

Anger Involves Passion

Anger causes many people to feel alive; it gives them a sense of safety and power. It makes them feel they can do something. Many women have discovered that moving from a position of passivity, vulnerability, helplessness and frustration to anger produces a wonderful sense of security, safety and power.

Anger Would Win the Prize as the Emotion "Most Likely to Be Mislabeled"

When people are asked, "When is the last time you remember experiencing anger?" they frequently have a difficulty remembering a specific time. Why? Since many people view anger only in its out-of-control form, they are unaware of the various ways the emotion of anger can be experienced and expressed in everyday life.

Because there are taboos on anger in many evangelical circles, Christians can be particularly blind to the value of this powerful emotion. Instead of identifying the emotion and facing it squarely as a fact of life, they either try to shut out and silence their anger or they allow it to dominate and control their lives.

Is there any emotion that people are encouraged to avoid as much as anger?

A person who is worried usually looks and acts worried. A person who is depressed usually looks and acts depressed. A person who is overcome by fear usually looks and acts afraid. But a person who is angry may or may not look and act angry. They may appear to be worried, depressed or afraid, or there may not be any external indication of their anger.

Of all the emotions anger is the one most likely to be labeled as something else. Of all the emotions anger is the one most likely to be identified as dangerous. What are some of the most common disguises anger can take? When we begrudge, scorn, insult, and disdain others or when we are annoyed, offended, bitter, fed up, repulsed, irritated, infuriated, incensed, mad, sarcastic, uptight, cross or when we experience frustration, indignation, exasperation, fury, wrath or rage, we are probably experiencing some form of anger. Anger can also manifest itself as criticism, silence, intimidation, hypochondria, numerous petty complaints, depression, gossip, sarcasm, blame, passive-aggressive behaviors such as stubbornness, half-hearted efforts, forgetfulness, and laziness.[3]

An important part of learning how to make our anger work for us is to be able to identify the many masks or disguises of anger.

Anger Is the Emotion "Most Likely to Be Blamed" for the Effects of Other Emotions

Think about it. Is there any other emotion that people are encouraged to avoid as much as anger? Is there any other emotion that is more likely to be labeled a sin? Is there any other emotion that people are more uncomfortable talking (or reading) about? This God-given emotion has a bad reputation.

The Faces of Anger

Let's take a look at some of the many different faces of anger.

Ire suggests greater intensity than anger, often with a clear physical display of feeling such as flushed cheeks or dilated pupils. *Rage* suggests loss of self-control leading to violence. *Fury* is a controlling and destructive rage that borders on madness. *Indignation* suggests a healthy anger at what one considers unfair, mean or shameful behavior.

When we don't deal with our anger, we are more likely to dwell on the causes. The more we focus on how we were wronged, the easier it is for the anger to turn into hostility. We want to punish, hurt or in some way repay the person who caused us the pain. Over time it's easy for the hostile thoughts to become aggression. Healthy anger lets others know exactly how you feel and why. It is honest and clear. Hostility is neither honest nor clear. The other people know they're in trouble but they're not sure why. They know they've done something wrong but they're not clear what.

Rage is much more than mere anger. It is anger under a pressure that seems to demand immediate action. There's no time to think about your anger. Rage demands to be acted upon. Anger influences but rage controls. If anger is a stream, then rage is a roaring river that's flooding over its banks.

The actions we take under the influence of rage are almost always *over*reactions. The rageaholic shouts, yells, screams, hits, hurls painful words, half-truths and sometimes objects, damages, destroys and then waltzes off into the sunset with no sense of guilt or remorse. Why? Because "they deserved it."

Anger and Hate

It's true that anger and hate are both emotions. But they are different emotions. Anger is not hate. Hate is not anger. Hate is the antonym of love. Anger is the antonym of apathy.

A careful study of the Bible reveals that there is a big difference between anger and hate. Psalm 106 provides a good example. In verse 40 we read, "The Lord was angry with His people." It is clear that the rebellion of His people caused the anger. But further reading shows this not to be the emotion of hate. The response is not of punishment, but of discipline and correction. Yes, the Lord did hand the Israelites over to their enemies. But in addition, "Many times he delivered them [and] he took note of their distress; . . . he remembered his covenant and out of his great love he relented" (Ps. 106:43-45, *NIV*). These are not acts of a raging and out-of-control God. Instead, God's anger arose out of His love. It was the means whereby God communicated His character. His sometimes painful discipline has its foundations in His love.

It's unfortunate that many people confuse the emotion of anger with the ways some people choose to express or act out that emotion. This confusion has caused anger to take the blame for some other emotions. Anger is not an evil emotion. The emotion of anger has never caused the breakup of a marriage, although inappropriate expressions of anger may have. Anger is not necessarily a dangerous or destructive emotion. Anger is not always a deadly sin. The problem lies in how we choose to express it.

Anger: A Learned Art

One woman wrote, "As a child the anger I knew was the stand-on-the-chair, yell-at-someone and throw-things kind of anger." Another woman wrote that "When I hear the word 'anger,' I think of coldness, sarcasm, contorted faces, slammed doors, extended silences, sobbing in back bedrooms, cold eyes and dark moods that kept everyone in the house on edge for days or weeks."

As men and women who are made in God's image, we are designed by our Creator to express ourselves. Given the fact that we are "born to communicate" it's surprising that clear communication is so difficult for so many people. I think there are two good reasons for this: original sin and our upbringing.

As part of their learning process children often imitate and then adopt the behavior patterns they see demonstrated in the adults around them. There are also external influences that contribute to a sense of what's considered appropriate behavior. These influences include friendships and role models picked up from television, movies and books.

A good example of this is the myth that it's more acceptable for women to express emotions than men. This starts at an early age when little children learn that it's OK for little girls to cry, but that a boy needs to "be a man." (And we all know that being a "real man" involves having emotional bypass surgery, that noninvasive procedure that takes place in childhood by which boys initially aware of their feelings learn to keep quiet about them.) After a while the child has suppressed his emotions for so long that he not only no longer recognizes them but also isn't even aware of them. By the time many boys become men they have lost the ability to express themselves. They have learned all too well that expressing emotions is not masculine and is thus unacceptable.

Mismanaged Anger

Mismanaged anger can be hazardous to your health.

What is mismanaged anger? It is anger that is not identified or understood and not dealt with in healthy kinds of ways. It is anger that is stuffed, repressed, suppressed, denied or ignored. It is out-of-control anger that keeps us from knowing what we are really feeling—and it does damage to ourselves and others.

What kind of damage? Consider these statistics from the American Academy of Family Physicians:

Women who bottle up their anger may be more likely than other women to have a heart attack by age 60, according to a report in *Psychosomatic Medicine*. In a 10-year follow-up study, 2,000 women who were enrolled in their 40s were followed until five years after menopause. The study showed that women who conceal their anger . . . have rising heart rates, levels of stress hormones and blood pressure, all of which have been linked to thickening of the carotid arteries.[4]

What's So Great About Anger?

In our survey of more than 3,000 women, we asked the question: When you hear the word "anger," do you tend to have a positive or a negative response to that word? In a random sample of more than 500 of the surveys, 77 percent of the respondents said, "Negative." We also asked: From your point of view, is anger primarily a positive or a negative emotion? Out of a random sample of 850 surveys, 78 percent of the respondents said, "Negative."

Yet as we have already mentioned, this oftentimes renegade emotion was designed by God as a gift and has tremendous potential for good. Let's take a look at some of the specific ways healthy anger can help us.

Anger is a signal. Anger is to our lives what a smoke detector is to a house or a dash warning light to a car. It serves as a warning to stop, look and listen. It says, "Caution; something may be wrong." In *The Dance of Anger*, Harriet Goldhor Lerner observes:

> Anger is a signal and one worth listening to. Our anger may be a message that we are being hurt, that our rights are being violated, that our needs or wants are not being adequately met, or simply that something isn't right. Our anger may tell us that we are not addressing an important emotional issue in our lives, or that too much of our self—our beliefs, values, desires or ambitions—is being compromised in a relationship. Our anger may be a signal that we are doing more and giving more than we can comfortably do or give. Or our anger may warn us that others are doing too much for us, at the expense of our own competence and growth. [5]

People who don't know how to listen to their anger are missing out on one of anger's greatest functions. As we learn to acknowledge anger's warning signs, we are more likely to be able to recognize and deal with an issue while it is still manageable.

When we don't recognize a problem issue or choose to ignore the warnings of anger, we are more likely to face bigger issues and greater problems down the road. When we ignore the warning lights of our emotions, what we might have been able to deal with fairly simply at an early stage will in time become a major problem.

Anger can provide a powerful source of motivation and energy to move us to positive action and change. Everyone wants to be different but nobody wants to change. Change is frustrating. Change is threatening. Change produces insecurity and increases our vulnerability to anxiety and fear. Change is one of the most difficult things in the world for most of us to accomplish. Yet change is what keeps us out of ruts. Without change there is no growth. Without growth there is psychological, spiritual or relational stagnation. Anger can be a prime catalyst for change.

> *As we learn to acknowledge anger's warning signs, we are more likely to be able to recognize and deal with an issue while it is still manageable.*

Managed anger can contribute to more intimate relationships. When most people hear the word "intimate," they think of safety, trust, transparency, security; of dealing with "someone who really knows me." They think of such people as a spouse or a best friend or bosom buddy. *Webster's Dictionary* defines "intimate" as "belonging to or characterizing one's deepest and most private nature."

True intimacy doesn't occur overnight. It takes time, a lot of it. Intimacy involves getting to know someone. It involves not only sharing the ways in which you are similar, but also sharing and working through your differences. It is through our differences that we reveal ourselves to one another as the unique persons God has made us to be. It is in working through our differences that we learn to understand and trust one another.

The emotion of anger is one of the most important ways we become aware of differences. Anger tells us that something is bothering us about another person. When this happens we can choose to move toward a surface or cosmetic harmony and pretend that everything is fine, or we can risk discomfort and awkwardness by speaking the truth in love, resolving the issue and in the process increasing the depth of the relationship.

> *The emotion of anger doesn't strengthen or weaken relationships—how we choose to express anger does.*

The road from not understanding to understanding often goes through the town of misunderstanding. Rarely are we able to communicate everything clearly the first time or understand someone else the first time, especially if it involves something as complex as emotions we don't always understand ourselves. (Sometimes it is only in the process of trying to communicate our feelings to someone else that we ourselves understand them.)

The emotion of anger doesn't strengthen or weaken relationships—how we choose to express anger does. If you choose to sit on your anger, the relationship is likely to remain shallow at best or, at worst, die a slow death. That is why a woman can come into my office and say, "I've been married to this man for 35 years and I have no idea who he is."

As we risk expressing and then moving beyond the secondary emotion of anger to its root causes, such as fear, hurt or frustration, we will be able to identify and grow beyond the differences that divide.

Anger can help us set boundaries and clarify who God has created us to be and to become. An important part of growing up is the establishment of personal boundaries. A personal boundary is part of what defines and distinguishes an individual. A personal boundary is where I leave off and you begin. My boundaries tell me that God has made me an individual with unique needs, wants, feelings, desires and dreams. Boundaries define appropriate behavior and expression of feelings. They let a person know when she is being violated or abused. They identify what is acceptable and unacceptable, appropriate and inappropriate.

Anger can be a warning that a personal boundary has been crossed, that you are being violated, abused or taken advantage of. It can give you the power to say no. Yet our surveys have shown that many women find it almost impossible to say no. Because they are not clear about who they are and who God created them to become, they direct most of their energy toward taking care of others and making them feel comfortable.

Not being able to say no makes a woman more vulnerable to becoming overresponsible. If a problem develops, she assumes it must be her fault. She spends much of her time apologizing for something she should have done, information she should have known or something she didn't do quite right. She has trained herself to take care of others, be mindlessly submissive, and follow everyone else's instructions, not only sacrificing her own needs but becoming substantially unaware of them so that she can more effectively cater to the needs of others.

One woman wrote, "I feel like my job is to function as the emotional thermostat for everyone else in the family." When that happens, you don't have any way to measure your own emotional climate. You deny your God-given talents and gifts. You are unaware of God's plan and purpose for your life.

Jesus never asked us to exchange our backbone for a wishbone. Being a godly woman doesn't mean not having your own ideas and options. A bumper sticker put it well: "Jesus died to take away our sins, not our brains." That means we are not to be conformed to what our family of origin, our spouse or our friends say we should be. As believers, we have the mind of Christ, and it is to Him that we are to become conformed.

Take Action

Dr. Redford Williams of Duke University has developed three questions that will help you identify if you are the kind of person whose hostility places her at risk of health problems down the road.[6] Answer the following questions by circling the answer that best describes you.

1. When friends or even strangers do things that hold me up or keep me from accomplishing a task, I often think they are selfish, mean and inconsiderate.

    Never   Sometimes   Often   Always

2. When someone does something that seems incompetent, messy, selfish or inconsiderate, I quickly feel frustration, irritation, anger or even rage. At the same time I often am aware of uncomfortable physical sensations such as a racing heart, being out of breath and sweating palms.

    Never   Sometimes   Often   Always

3. Whenever I have those kinds of thoughts, feelings or bodily sensations, I am more likely to communicate my feelings to the person I see as the cause of my discomfort with words, gestures, a change in my tone of voice or negative facial expressions.

    Never   Sometimes   Often   Always

Dr. Williams's research has shown that if you answer "Often" or "Always" to two of the three survey items, it is probable that your level of hostility places you in a high-risk group for health problems. You may have what Dr. Williams calls a hostile heart.

WHAT ARE EMOTIONS, ANYWAY?

Gary J. Oliver

A recently divorced mother of two asked me during a counseling session, "Dr. Oliver, I know I'm supposed to be an expert on emotions, but right now I have no idea what I'm feeling—except bad."

"Carol," I said, "who told you that you are supposed to be an expert on emotions?"

She responded, "Well, everyone knows that women are more emotional than men."

Carol represents the thousands of women we have worked with and surveyed. They believed that because they were women they should somehow magically understand and be experts on their emotions—not just their own emotions, but also the emotions of everyone around them.

They were the subtle victims of some of the widespread misbeliefs about women, men and emotions. In their extreme form some of these misbeliefs include:

- God designed women to be more emotional than men.
- God designed women to have different emotions than men.
- God designed women to feel but not think. He made men to think but not feel.
- God designed women to be right-brained. He made men to be left-brained.
- God designed women to be nurturing. He made men to be competitive.

A woman psychologist stated, "It is a myth to believe that women are always in touch with our feelings—or that we have any more of them than men do. One of the strongest feelings that every human has encountered during his or her lifetime is anger. . . . We [women] do not always easily express much of anger."[1]

What Exactly Are Emotions?

In the first chapter we introduced the issue of anger, its causes and some of the ways we can handle it. Later, we will consider depression, fear and anxiety. But in order to understand and deal with all of these, we must first understand what emotions are, where they come from, how God designed them to function, how sin has damaged them and what we can do about them. We need to know the relative importance of emotions and when we can trust them and when we cannot. We need to know how feelings relate to thinking and how much weight to give to each one. These are some of the matters we will deal with in this chapter.

Webster defines "emotion" as "a psychic and physical reaction subjectively experienced as strong feeling and physiologically involving changes that prepare the body for immediate vigorous action." The English word "emotion" is derived from the Latin word *emovare* which means "to move" or "having to do with motion, movement and energy."

Dorothy Finkelhor, author of *How to Make Your Emotions Work for You*, says emotions are

the motivating forces of our lives, driving us to go ahead, pushing us backward, stopping us completely, determining what we do, how we feel, what we want, and whether we get what we want. Our hates, loves, fears, and what to do about them are determined by our emotional structure. There is nothing in our lives that does not have the emotional factor as its mainspring. It gives us power, or makes us weak, operates for our benefit or to our detriment, for our happiness or confusion.[2]

In Psalm 139:14 the psalmist states, "I am fearfully and wonderfully made" (*NIV*). Nowhere is the delicate complexity of God's creation more evident than in our emotional makeup. Our emotions are complex. The experience of emotions involve sensory, skeletal, motor, autonomic and cognitive aspects. Our emotions influence the spiritual, social, intellectual and physical parts of our lives.

What Are Some of the Most Common Emotions?

In seminars and workshops I've asked participants to make a list of frequently experienced emotions. Here are some of the most frequently listed emotions.

Acceptance	Elation	Hurt
Anger	Embarrassment	Indifference
Anxiety	Excitement	Loneliness
Appreciation	Fear	Love
Boredom	Fright	Pride
Concern	Frustration	Sadness
Confidence	Generosity	Shame
Confusion	Gladness	Surprise
Delight	Grief	Terror
Depression	Happiness	Ticked
Discomfort	Humiliation	Worry

Characteristics of Emotions

If we are to move toward emotional maturity there are certain characteristics of emotions that are important for us to be aware of. One of the most helpful ways to understand emotions is to look at some characteristics that emotions have in common.

All of Our Emotions Were Created by God

The best place to start is where the Bible starts, and that's with Creation.

> Then God said, "Let us make man in our image in our likeness, and let them rule over the fish of the sea and the birds of the air, over the livestock, over all the earth, and over all the creatures that move along the ground" (Gen. 1:26, *NIV*).

When God made us in His image He gave us a mind, a will and emotions. Our mind gives us the ability to think. Our emotions provide the ability to feel. Our will allows the opportunity to choose. He intentionally designed these three parts of our person to work together in balance and harmony. Like the legs of a three-legged milking stool, each dimension of our personality is important and necessary. They are intricately interrelated. The choices we make influence what we feel. Our emotions influence what we think and the decisions that we make. Our thoughts influence how we feel and the choices we make.

When our mind and emotions work together, we are more likely to make wise choices.

Our emotions and our minds are two different yet equally valuable ways of experiencing and understanding life. They provide us with two different kinds of information about ourselves and the world around us. They can balance each other out. When our mind and emotions work together, we are more likely to make wise choices.

Although God designed these three to work in harmony, sin has seriously complicated the picture. Sin brought a division between God and humanity. It brought a division between male and female. And it produced a division within each one of us.

Due to the Fall and the effects of sin in our lives, our mind, will and emotions have become damaged and distorted. The division is especially evident in relation to our mind and our emotions. God designed them to work together in a complimentary relationship, but now they often oppose each other. One of the many effects of sin has been to produce in each of us a tendency to prefer one over the other, sometimes even to the exclusion of the other.

Error #1: Mind over emotions. Those who emphasize the mind believe that emotions are untrustworthy and unreliable. I heard one well-known preacher state that "You can't base your decisions on your emotions. Emotions change, but God's Word never changes. There is no room for emotionalism in the mature Christian life." With good intentions this pastor built an artificial and unbiblical dichotomy between the mind and emotions, saying the mind is good and the emotions are bad.

He viewed emotions as a necessary evil. It's probably good to be aware of them but one shouldn't take them too seriously. When it comes to making decisions, ignore your feelings. They are fickle, changeable, unreliable—and they only get you into trouble. Only people who don't know how to think rely on their emotions.

Unfortunately, many evangelicals have bought into this error. Emotions are the "black sheep" of our personality. Emotions are at best unimportant and at worst a mark of immaturity.

Even people [who believe] that Jesus was fully human may assume that Jesus transcended emotion. Believers who grow up in a community of faith that is suspicious of emotion may view Jesus through that predetermined lens and imagine that he was too "good," or too "perfect," to have emotions.[3]

I've worked with many men who believe that if they feel strongly about what they're saying, even if they can't give good reasons for it, they're being rational. Or course from their perspective if a woman does the same thing, she is being irrational, illogical and, even worse, emotional. Why? Because she is a woman.

If you carry this error a bit further you can end up with the even more absurd conclusion that, since the mind is more reliable than emotions, and since men are better at thinking than feeling, therefore the gender orientation known as masculinity is by definition better and more reliable than femininity. It's hard to believe that people actually believe this, but they do.

When we elevate the mind to a position of superiority and relegate the emotions to the servants' quarters we are splitting our personality in ways God never intended. We are trading in our emotional birthright for an intellectual mess of pottage. This is a trade God never asks us to make.

Error #2: Emotions over mind. For some people, emotions are the measuring stick of life. All feelings are factual and valid. They have the final word. Their motto is "If I don't feel like it, I shouldn't do it. God doesn't want me to be a phony." Those who emphasize the mind are viewed as hard, cold, insensitive, unkind and uncaring. Their only concern is for the "bottom line." For them, things are much more important than people.

This error was well illustrated by a cartoon showing a husband and wife in an argument. The wife turns to the husband and says, "Anyone who has to resort to logic must be pretty unsure of himself."

Feelings are important. But they were never meant to be the absolute standard of truth, the infallible guide to what is right, the source of all our decisions and actions.

C. S. Lewis wrote that "No natural feelings are high or low, holy or unholy in themselves. They are all holy when God's hand is on the rein. They all go bad when they set up on their own and make themselves into false Gods."[4]

Which of the two errors is most characteristic of how you function? Where did you learn that this was the "right" way to be? How about your same-sex parent and your opposite-sex parent? If you are married which is most characteristic of your spouse?

Both of these errors reveal a major misunderstanding of the biblical teaching on how God designed us to function. True spiritual maturity involves the whole person. It is impossible to be spiritually mature and emotionally or intellectually immature. It's not a matter of mind over emotions or emotions over mind. True maturity involves a balance between our heart, head and will; among our feeling, thinking and doing. Each is important. Each was designed by God for our good. Each is a manifestation of the image of God in us.

All of Us Have Emotions

It doesn't matter if you are male or female, young or old, black or white, rich or poor—we all experience and, to a greater or lesser degree, express emotions. We all have the capacity to experience the full range of emotions.

One of the misbeliefs of emotions is that there are male and female emotions. Recently I've had several women tell me, in a humorous vein, that men have only two emotions: lust and anger. At the same time I've had several men, in a more serious vein, tell me that there are male emotions and female emotions.

Emotions Aren't Good or Bad, Healthy or Unhealthy

One of the most dangerous misconceptions of emotions is that there some emotions are good and some aren't. Emotions can be experienced as negative or positive, painful or pleasurable but here aren't any "bad" emotions. There are only bad or unhealthy expressions of them.

Emotions Have a Physical Effect

I can't count the number of times I've heard a sincere (though sincerely wrong) person say to his or her spouse, "Honey, it's all in your head." That is one of the most common misbeliefs of emotions is that "it's all in your head." Emotions are in our head, but they're in the rest of our body as well.

The experience of emotions involve changes in our central and peripheral nervous systems that include a variety of chemicals and neurotransmitters. When you experience emotions your heart may beat faster, the pupil in your eyes may dilate, you may have increased perspiration, you may tremble, tears may come to your eyes, you may get goose bumps, and you might experience a tremendous surge of energy or you could feel totally drained.

Not only is there a powerful physiological component to our emotions, but how we deal with our emotions can also have a positive or negative effect on our health. For many years medical research has documented the role that a misuse of emotions can play in the disease process. However, until now little had been said about the potential role emotions can play in the process of healing.

The findings of an increasing number of studies is showing that the healthy use of emotions can aid in the healing and recovery process.

If We Understand and Control Our Emotions, We Can Make Them Work for Us Rather Than Against Us

It doesn't matter how important or unimportant we think our emotions are. It doesn't matter how much we are aware of them. Whether we like it or not, for better or for worse, they play a major role in our lives. One thing is quite clear. If we don't understand and control our emotions they will control us.

> *It doesn't matter how important or unimportant we think our emotions are. Whether we like it or not, for better or for worse, they play a major role in our lives.*

Some people suffer from the disease of overcontrolled emotions. When we are out of touch with our emotions we are out of touch with our true needs. We become "other-focused" in the unhealthy sense of the word. Gradually we lose a sense of our selves and can become emotionally dependent on and addicted to others.

It can get to the point that we allow others to define who we are. In these kinds of relationships our significance and security are determined not by who we are in Christ, not by what He accomplished for us on the cross, not by what God has to say about us. The basis for our sense of significance and security is determined by the "significant other" in our lives.

These individuals tend to gravitate toward dependent-independent relationships. Here are some of the characteristics of those individuals:

The Self	The Other
is emotionally overavailable	is emotionally unavailable
focuses on others	focuses on themselves
gives encouragement, support, money, time, etc.	gives little, if anything, to to anyone
their needs are rarely met	their needs are being met
gives much more than 50 percent	gives much less that 50 percent
gives up or loses power	maintains and gains power
validates the other	is validated by others
tolerates inappropriate behavior	often engages in inappropriate behavior
attaches or becomes enmeshed with the other	detaches or moves away (disengaged) from the other[5]

According to women leaders we surveyed, this is a special problem for women. In the dependent-independent relationships, do you know who is most often in the "dependent" role? That's right. The woman. Some women have an advanced case of overcontrolled emotions.

The opposite of the overcontrolled individual is the emotionally out-of control person. These are the ones we tend to hear about on the news and read about in the paper. It's clear that when we let the river of emotion get out of control it can flood its banks and wreak havoc. Some people are both. Most of the time they are overcontrolled but, every now and then, they get out-of-control. Being close to a person like that makes life, at best, chaotic. A roller coaster is a lot of fun to ride on. But I wouldn't want to try to live on one of them. Being married to a person who swings from overcontrolled emotions to out-of-control emotions is like trying to live on a roller coaster.

Emotional Maturity Can Increase Our Effectiveness

Dr. Alice Isen, a psychologist at the University of Maryland, has spent more than 17 years studying the ways in which positive emotions affect the way people think. Her research suggests that positive emotions not only make people more helpful and generous toward others but also appear to improve thinking processes such as judgment, problem solving, decision making and creativity.

She said, "Good feelings seem capable of bringing out our better nature socially and our creativity in thinking and problem-solving . . . are a potential source of interpersonal cooperativeness and personal health and growth. Our studies have implications for classrooms, businesses, relationships or any situation where you want to bring out the best in someone." "Positive emotions," Isen says, "encourage people to look beyond the normal problem-solving method to try different options."[6]

Shared Emotions Are the Currency of Healthy Relationships

Our research has shown that women like to talk about emotions more than men do. That wasn't any big surprise. It simply confirmed the results of other research we've seen. Women reported that the emotional quality of a relationship seemed more important to them than to their husbands. They say that talking about their emotions helps them sort out their feelings and express closeness.

Actually shared emotions aren't only important for women. For all of us, female and male, emotions need to be communicated.

"Emotional" Is Not a Dirty Word

What do you think of when you hear the word "emotional"? Is your first response a positive or a negative one? Has anyone ever called you "emotional"? Do you remember the last time it happened? What was the context? Were they giving you a compliment? Did you respond by saying "Thank you. I'm so pleased that you noticed"? Or did you take it as a criticism or put-down? Was the person who labeled your behavior emotional a man or a woman? Does the gender of the person using the word "emotional" affect how you interpret its meaning?

When most people use the word "emotional," they are referring to someone's behavior. "Stop being so emotional." "You are starting to sound emotional." It's also used to describe an enduring characteristic of a person. "She is just an emotional person."

There doesn't seem to be any clear definition for the word "emotional." Its definition is influenced by the behavior of the person who is being described and the intentions of the one who is doing the labeling. Being emotional has something to do with the frequency, intensity, duration and appropriateness of a response.

What is clear is that the label "emotional" is most often used in a negative context. It's often used in an attempt to influence or control a person's behavior. An emotional person is often considered irresponsible, immature and irrational. We've done a word association with several women's groups for the word "emotional" and some of the words they find most frequently associated with it include "out of control," "immature," "irresponsible," "irrational" and "childish."

Several years ago the *San Francisco Chronicle* conducted a survey of their male readers' opinions about women. The survey was designed to reveal what men want and don't want from women. What came out in front of the men's complaints were frustrations regarding women's emotional behavior. Women's nagging was first, with 44 percent of the respondents listing it as their major irritation. The second most common problem with a 39 percent response was that "women get too emotional when I argue."

One writer asked: "Why is it 'arguing' when he does it, but 'getting emotional' when she does it? Why does the word 'nagging' immediately bring to mind the picture of an unstable woman building toward an emotional tirade?"[7]

While this wasn't a rigorous scientific survey it did tap into one of the most common gender stereotypes. Men are portrayed as calm, cool and rational, even in the face of great danger. Their emotional displays are limited to righteous anger and golly-gosh-gee-shucks tongue-tied expressions of love. While she, on the other hand, swoons with emotions at the slightest provocation. She'll even cry over television commercials. Emotions, of all qualities and quantities, are her trademark. It doesn't seem to matter that there are numerous exceptions to that stereotype. It is still alive and well.

Take Action

Completing the following statements will give you better insight into your emotional responses.

Emotions Check Up

1. The emotions I express most easily are . . .
2. The emotions I saw my mother express were . . .
3. The emotions I saw my father express were . . .
4. The emotion that bothers me most is . . .
5. What depresses me is . . .
6. My greatest fear is . . .
7. What I worry about most is . . .
8. When I am depressed I . . .
9. A positive effect of my emotions is . . .
10. One change I would like to make in my emotions is . . .

CHAPTER 4

WHY IS ANGER THE FORBIDDEN EMOTION?

Gary J. Oliver

"Somehow when I was a little girl I learned that anger was the forbidden emotion. Especially for little girls." With a halting voice and misty eyes Janet, a 42-year-old mother continued, "Whenever I expressed anger as a child my parents would emotionally withdraw from me." At an early age she learned that love was based on her performance. It was conditional. When she expressed anger, love was removed. It didn't take long for her to associate expressing anger with abandonment and rejection.

The unconscious lesson Janet learned was "If I express anger, I won't be loved." She concluded that it didn't pay to express anger, and she learned to fear her anger. Instead of learning how to use her anger to clarify and strengthen her own identity, she learned how to pursue excellence in ignoring her anger. She discovered that what did pay was learning how to "read" people and give them what they wanted. She became a people-pleaser. She learned how to perform. Everyone referred to her as a "nice girl."

What brought Janet into counseling was that now, as an adult, she found it was becoming harder and harder to control her temper. "Things will go along great for several weeks and then, sometimes over the tiniest provocation, I will lose it," she told me. At first it would build gradually. "But lately, all of a sudden I find myself shouting, screaming, snapping at my kids or lashing out at Larry. I look at the way I am traumatizing my family, and I feel guilt and shame. After each episode I feel terrible about myself. I bend over backward to make up for what I've done. I ask them to forgive me. Yet with each succeeding episode, it becomes harder for them to trust me. They're scared because they never know when I'm going to lose it. It becomes harder for me to trust myself. I feel like I'm doing damage to my husband, my kids and myself."

Janet had spent a lifetime burying her anger and now, like an emotional volcano, the pressure was getting too strong. Because she had never learned how to understand and control or direct her anger it was now starting to control her.

Janet's experience is not unique. In our surveys we asked women "what emotion is the most difficult for you to express?" To an overwhelming degree the number one response was anger. For many years women have been discouraged from the awareness and clear expression of anger. Anger has become, in Janet's words, "the forbidden emotion."

Harriet Goldhor Lerner has written,

Sugar and Spice are the ingredients from which we are made. We are the nurturers, the soothers, the peacemakers, and the steadiers of rocked boats. It is our job to please, protect, and placate the world. We may hold relationships in place as if our lives depended on it.[1]

Seven Misbeliefs About Anger

Janet, like many of us, had been raised to accept certain beliefs about anger. Unfortunately, most of them were wrong. Of all the emotions, anger is the least understood and most misunderstood—and it's not just women who have been raised with misbeliefs and misunderstandings about it. All of us have. Some misbeliefs, however, have had a much more negative effect on women. Based on our clinical experience and the results of our surveys and interviews we have identified seven misbeliefs about anger that have had a particularly damaging effect on women.

Misbelief #1: The Bible Teaches That Anger Is a Sin

According to this misbelief, anger should be "put away" or avoided—and further, whenever we allow ourselves to get angry we are sinning.

This misbelief is one of the most dangerous and absurd of them all. Yet many people believe it. I read it in books, I see it in the lives of people I know, I hear it on the radio and in the counseling room.

"I really don't have anything to be angry and depressed about," Patti said with a deep sigh. "That's why these emotions are so confusing. I know I shouldn't feel this way. But I do!" Patti had asked to see me for help in understanding and dealing with her increasing anger and resentment toward her husband and children.

Patti and Roger had been married for eight years. They had two preschoolers and one seven-year-old. Roger was a committed husband and father. He held a good-paying job but was "on the road" a lot. As we talked it became clear that Patti was frustrated with her life. "I love being a wife and a mother but is this all there is? There's got to be something more."

If you were the counselor how would you view Patti's situation? What is the problem? What approach would you take? What is the biblical perspective? Here are two different ways of looking at her situation:

If you believe in misbelief #1, you would probably say that Patti's anger is unhealthy, inappropriate and caused by her sin nature or spiritual immaturity. Patti had talked with a speaker at a women's conference who took this approach. She told Patti that she should be grateful for a husband who was a good provider and for three healthy children.

However, it's possible that much of Patti's anger is healthy, legitimate, appropriate and realistic. With the best of intentions she had slipped into a view of motherhood that relegated her to living vicariously through her husband and her children. Her experience of anger was a sign that something was wrong and needed to be discussed. She believed that a "good mother" always puts everyone's needs ahead of her own, even to the exclusion of her own. But serving doesn't mean selling out. It doesn't have to be either-or; it can be both-and.

The apostle Paul challenges this misbelief when he says: "Be angry, and yet do not sin; do not let the sun go down on your anger, and do not give the devil an opportunity" (Eph. 4:26-27, *NASB*). Do be angry but don't sin. The first word Paul uses for anger (*orge*) refers to a attitude of anger which is slow in its onset. But when he says "do not let the sun go down on your anger," he uses a word for anger (*parorgismos*) that refers to a stronger form of anger that is characterized by irritation and exasperation. Paul makes it very clear that while it is normal to experience anger, we can choose to express that anger in ways that are not sinful.

It's not a sin to experience anger. However, sin can enter the picture when we don't acknowledge and deal with our anger. If we allow it to lead to bitterness, resentment, an unforgiving spirit or the tendency to make others "pay" for their wrongs, we are more likely to express our anger in sinful kinds of ways.

> *It's not a sin to experience anger. However, sin can enter the picture when we don't acknowledge and deal with our anger.*

One of the most basic errors of the anger misbeliefs is the failure to make a distinction between experiencing the emotion of anger and the ways in which we choose to express it. This error plagues many people and keeps them from fully understanding, appreciating and being able to use this God-given emotion in ways that help and heal rather than in ways that hurt.

As we mature, God wants to teach us how to balance the emotion of anger with other emotions. In Exodus 34:6 God is described as a "compassionate and gracious God, slow to anger, abounding in love and faithfulness" (*NIV*). The Bible reveals a God who experiences and expresses anger. But He also balances His anger with other emotions such as gentleness, kindness, compassion, loving-kindness and truth.

Misbelief #2: If You Don't Look or Sound Angry, You Don't Have a Problem with Anger

This misbelief makes the assumption that whenever we experience an emotion that we are probably aware of it and cannot help but show it on our face. It is true that some individuals have a difficult time hiding what they feel. Even a stranger can look them and tell what is going on inside. But there are a lot of people for whom this is not the case.

Over the years I've found that, at times, anger can be caught peeking out from behind other safer and more innocuous expressions. Here is a sample of some that I've collected over the years. They represent what we say instead of, "I'm angry!"

You always . . .	You never . . .
I'm down in the dumps.	I wish that . . .
I'm disappointed.	I just don't understand why.
It's not fair that . . .	I'm depressed.
You should/shouldn't . . .	I'm feeling blue.
I'm sick and tired of . . .	When will you ever . . .
I'm sorry.	I'm fed up.

People use these expressions when they are angry but are not aware of it or, if they are, they have learned to repress, suppress, deny or ignore it.

Misbelief #3: Nice Girls Don't Get Angry—And If They Do Get Angry, They Don't Express It

Historically, women have been led to believe that it is wrong for them to experience anger. Victorian women, for example, were not supposed to even feel anger. Anger and femininity were antithetical. One Victorian author, describing his angry wife, said that, "every womanly emotion—generosity—delicacy—honor—yielded before the demon that held her in his iron fold" and that temper "stifled the exercise of every womanly and gentle feeling." Experiencing the emotion of anger has nothing to do with being naughty or nice.

The women we surveyed gave us some additional characteristics of "nice girls." Not only do nice girls not get angry, nice girls are weak, nice girls don't have opinions, and nice girls don't disagree, especially with men and most especially on theological issues.

The underlying thread in all of these "misbeliefs" is that being "nice" means staying in the background, being seen but not heard, not making any waves, and making men look good and appear smart and strong. They all reflect our society's discomfort with strong women. Therapist Celia Halas says,

> [Anger] is an emotion that women express far less frequently than do men. In fact, men generally feel quite comfortable with anger, express it freely, and are reasonably careless about the problems it causes in other people. . . . Women are generally afraid to express their anger. They have been taught that to do so is unladylike.[2]

Men and women do differ in how they express love, anger and other emotions. However, this difference isn't because women are naturally "emotional" and men are naturally "rational" or, as one woman put it, "because women are naturally 'open' and men are by nature 'emotionally brain-dead.'" Research has found few differences between men and women in the kinds of emotions they feel or in how intensely they feel them. Many differences in how men and women express emotions result from cultural expectations. Women are expected, allowed and required to reveal certain emotions, and men are expected, and required to deny or suppress them.[3]

For many people expressions of anger and assertiveness are still considered masculine in men, and unfeminine in women. There continue to be strong societal prohibitions against female anger. For many women these prohibitions create deep unconscious anxieties about expressing themselves, disagreeing with men, being assertive or competitive.

Unlike male heroes who fight and even die for what they believe in, the angry or aggressive woman may, indeed, repel us all. For what images come to mind? The envious, castrating "man-hater" venting her rage and resentment against men? The passive-aggressive housewife who bit-terly dominates and controls her husband from behind the scenes? The infantile, irrational, "hot-tempered" female who hurls pots and pans from across the kitchen and carries on like a hysterical bitch? These familiar images are more than just cruel, sexist stereotypes.[4]

Nice people love. Nice people are compassionate. Nice people are concerned. Nice people can be discouraged. Nice people experience hurt, frustration and fear. Nice people experience anger. Nice people express their anger in healthy kinds of ways.

Misbelief #4: Getting Angry Is Always Selfish

Many women in our culture have been conditioned to be the caretakers, the custodians of relationships. Their job is to think of, watch out for and take care of others. If they do a good enough job taking care of everyone else then maybe, just maybe, someone will take care of them, provide for their happiness and satisfy their God-given needs.

In Philippians 2:3 Paul writes, "Let each regard the others as better than and superior to himself—thinking more high-ly of one another than you do of your-selves" (*AMP*). Every person is of infinite worth and value deserves to honored.

But the fact that others are important does not mean that we are unimportant. God is not glorified when we trample and ignore who He has created us to be. God "made him [Christ] who knew no sin to be sin on our behalf, that we might become the righteousness of God in him" (2 Cor. 5:21, *NASB*) and "partakers of the divine nature" (2 Pet. 1:4, *NASB*). Moreover, believers are "beholding as in a mirror the glory of the Lord, [and] are being transformed into the same image" (2 Cor. 3:18, *NASB*).

The healthy expression of legitimate anger can be a statement of dignity and self-respect.

Getting angry can indeed be selfish. It's easy for anyone to get angry for the wrong reasons. Pride, jealousy, selfishness, being preoccupied with "me" and insensitive toward "you"—these are all unhealthy causes of anger.

But anger isn't *necessarily* selfish. The healthy expression of legitimate anger can be a statement of dignity and self-respect. It can also be a statement that what I believe in is so important that I am willing to take the risk of standing alone, even in the face of disapproval, rejection or the threatened lost of support from those I love.

Misbelief #5: Anger Usually Leads to Some Form of Violence and Therefore It Is Never Good to Be Angry

Erika was proud to be able to state that she was not an angry person and that, as far as she knew, she rarely even experienced the emotion of anger. Yet she did admit that she was frequently forgetful, tended to avoid problems, was often late, liked to change the subject and was skilled in the use of subtle sarcasm.

In providing a brief history of her family of origin, Erika indicated that her father had been an alcoholic. "I would listen for the sound of his voice and a certain look on his face. Certain nonverbal signs always told me whether or not he would be beating Mom that night. I always knew if I had to gather my brothers and sisters up and get them out of the way. Whenever Dad got angry, he would either beat on Mom or one of us kids."

At an early age, Erika had learned to equate anger and violence. Since she had vowed to herself that she would never be like her father, she simply denied any feelings of anger. She thought that if she never got angry she would never be violent. Over a period of several months Erika learned how to distinguish between the experience of anger and the various ways in which anger can be expressed.

She had frequently experienced the emotion of anger, she had simply found different ways to express it. While her passive and indirect expressions of anger were not as violent as her father's active and direct expressions of it, both ways of dealing with the anger were unhealthy. Erika's denial of anger served to obscure and hide her deepest hurts and needs and concerns from herself and from those she loved.

Misbelief #6: Since God Is Love and Anger Is the Opposite of Love, It Is Clear That God Is Against Anger

I've often heard the statement that anger is the opposite of love—that anger and love don't mix. I disagree. Anger isn't the opposite of love. We can choose to express our anger in ways that are unkind and unloving. However, I believe that the real opposite of love is indifference.

Indifference doesn't care, doesn't let itself care. It sits back, waits, watches, plays it safe. It doesn't give, doesn't invest, doesn't get involved, doesn't take risks. Indifference isn't hot or cold; it is luke-warm.

This misbelief says that "If you love me you won't get angry with me." The truth is that a loving relationship includes the freedom for each partner to experience and express their emotions. *All* of them. The fun ones and the painful ones. In a healthy relationship anger is not only permitted, it is encouraged.

Healthy anger can be a powerful and legitimate tool for communicating love. Healthy anger says something or someone is valuable, important and worth protecting. The truth is that you can't have real love without some anger. One of the questions for a healthy relationship is, Do we love and trust each other enough to believe that it is really OK to be angry?

In the sometimes delightful process of two individuals becoming one it is inevitable that there will be differences. On one hand, those differences are what brought us together. On the other hand, those differences are the source of our greatest frustration and pain. Those differences provide the strength and balance in the relationship. The process of negotiating those differences is what allows our hearts to be knit together as one, to experience the breadth and depth of what true love can be.

Anger and love are separate emotions, but the deeper the caring, the deeper the potential for frustration and hurt and then anger. By not being in touch with and communicating our anger to each other we don't allow our family or friends to understand our hurts and frustrations. By not sharing our hurts and frustrations we rob each other of the opportunity to better understand each other.

Misbelief #7: If I Express My Anger, I Will Be Shamed, Punished or Rejected

Some women don't express their anger because they fear retaliation. They fear that admitting their anger will result in abandonment, punishment, revenge or loss of love. One woman said, "If I express my anger, I'll pay for it. It may be sooner or later, but I'll pay for it." Therefore many women have never learned to understand their God-given emotion of anger and thus don't know how to express it in healthy and constructive ways.

> *Women fear that admitting their anger will result in abandonment, punishment, revenge or loss of love.*

What are some of the fears or concerns you have in regard to the emotion of anger? Women in a workshop generated the following responses to the question "When I imagine being angry directly, I fear . . ."

losing control	losing my job
not being liked	scaring or hurting someone
getting physically hurt	losing my credibility
being called weak	being labeled defensive
being laughed at	feeling guilty
being called overemotional	being labeled unprofessional[5]

Many of the women we surveyed reported feeling shamed for even having their own needs and emotions, especially the emotion of anger. Many women said that they still feel guilt and shame when they experience anger. Those painful feelings increase when they assert themselves by saying no or by stating what they need or want.

Webster's Dictionary defines "shame" as "a disturbed or painful feeling of guilt, incompetence, indecency or blameworthiness." In our experience this emotion can range from a slight embarrassment to deep humiliation, self-depreciation, self-hate and even suicidal thoughts.

Healthy shame tells me that I *did* something wrong. Unhealthy shame tells me that I *am* wrong. A person who evaluates his or her behavior from a healthy shame-base is motivated to learn from a mistake and do something different. A person coming from a toxic shame-base sees their mistake as further evidence that he or she is a mistake. No matter what such a person does, it will never be enough. Despair and discouragement replace hope.

At times the experience of anger can cause us to feel separate, different or alone. The expression of anger involves stating the differences between people. Even a healthy expression of anger involves standing on your own two feet, being clear about what is important, being separate and apart from the other people for a time.

When all is said and done there is some truth to this mistaken idea. If we allow ourselves to be vulnerable, we may be taken advantage of. If we show our concern and compassion for others and expose our emotions, someone may interpret it as incompetence and dump on us. If you express your anger, you may be shamed, punished or rejected. It is a real risk.

But it is probable that you have experienced shame, punishment or rejection even when you haven't expressed your anger. Allowing your fear of those responses to control your behavior keeps you a prisoner of other people's irresponsible behavior. It reinforces their immaturity. And it removes any hope of meaningful communication, understanding and growth.

Through a healthy expression of your anger, you have a greater likelihood of accurately communicating what you really think and how strongly you feel about certain issues. An appropriate expression of anger is much more likely to move the issue into a place where it can be clearly seen, acknowledged and understood. This provides the basis for resolution of conflicts and the ability to move ahead in a relationship.

Take Action

Listed below are the seven common misconceptions about anger that may sneak into your thought-life or behavior. In the space underneath each misbelief, write in your own words the *truth* about this aspect of anger.

1. The Bible teaches that anger is a sin and something that should be "put away" or avoided—and whenever we allow ourselves to get angry, we are sinning.
2. If you don't look or sound angry, you don't have a problem with anger.
3. Nice girls don't get angry, and if they do get angry, they don't express it.
4. Getting angry is always selfish.
5. Anger usually leads to some form of violence; and, therefore, it is never good to be angry.
6. Since God is love and anger is the opposite of love, it is clear that God is against anger.
7. If I express anger, I will be shamed, punished or rejected.

How Do You "Do" Anger?

Gary J. Oliver

Anger comes packaged in a variety of shapes and sizes. It hides behind many different masks. Each of us has developed our own unique style of dealing with anger. In the previous chapter we surveyed several common anger problems. Now we're going to focus on three major anger styles that amplify some of those problems.

Not long ago I asked a group of women to call out some of the words they've heard people use to describe the experience and expression of anger. Before they were done I had filled two sheets of paper. Here are some of the words they came up with:

Affront	Begrudge	Cranky
Aggravated	Bitter	Cross
Agitated	Bristle	Despise
Annoyed	Burned-up	Disdain
Animosity	Catty	Disgusted
Aroused	Criticize	Enraged
Bad Blood	Cool	Exasperated

Exploded	Ill-will	Resentment
Frustrated	Irritated	Riled
Fed Up	Infuriated	Sarcastic
Fume	Inflamed	Scorned
Furious	Indignation	Seethe
Grieved	Jealous	Slow burn
Grumpy	Mad	Spiteful
Grouchy	Mean	Steamed
Gripe	Miffed	Stew
Hateful	Moody	Temper
Hostile	Out of sorts	Touchy
Hot	Offended	Tiff
Huffy	Provoked	Vexed
Hurt	Rage	Vicious
Irked	Rant	Wounded
Incensed	Rave	Worked-up
Ill-tempered	Repulsed	Wrath

Then I asked them to come up with a list of phrases some people use to describe the experience and expression of anger. Some of the most common phrases included:

Blew up	Flew into a rage	Swallow your anger
Blow off steam	Get it off your chest	Totally lost it
Boiling mad	Hot under the collar	Went ballistic
Defuse your anger	Raised her hackles	
Did a slow burn	Simmer down	
Fired up	Storming mad	

As children we experienced events that elicited an anger response. Over time what may have started out as a conscious reaction became, with many repetitions, an automatic and unconscious reaction. Because these reactions appear to be so natural, many people believe they are a part of who they are. They see these styles as part of how God made them rather than styles that have been learned and thus can be changed, with God's help.

The first and easiest step in the change process is to identify your characteristic style of experiencing and expressing anger. When it comes to dealing with anger, most people tend to fall into one of three reactive styles. A person who is reactive has an automatic and seemingly unconscious response to a situation. She may not always react in the exact same way but the majority of their responses fall into similar styles.

People who don't identify and work on their anger style are in an emotional rut and likely to stay there. They are vulnerable to becoming puppets of their past and slaves to their circumstances.

Some of the women I've worked with have given very descriptive names to these three unhealthy styles. As you read about them, think of which one might best describe your usual way of reacting.

> *People who don't identify and work on their anger style are in an emotional rut and likely to stay there.*

Cream Puffs

Patty walked into my office and told me in a very quiet tone of voice that she wasn't sure why she was there. "If my doctors hadn't insisted I come for a few visits, I never would have come on my own." Patty had gone to see her physician for some stomach problems and difficulty sleeping. He couldn't find anything wrong and so he referred her to several specialists. Finally he referred her to me because he and several other specialists she had consulted concluded that there was no physiological cause for her problems.

As Patty told me her story, it was clear that a part of her problem was her misunderstanding of the emotion of anger and her inability to deal with it. At one point she turned to me and said, "I'm just a cream puff. I look great on the outside, but I feel like I don't have much substance, I can't handle any pressure. I collapse easily." I told Patty she wasn't alone. Many women, and even some men, would describe themselves as "cream puffs."

Mary Kay Biaggio, program director and professor at the Oregon Graduate School of Professional Psychology, has studied anger for nearly 10 years. Her research has demonstrated that although women experience anger in response to many of the same situations as men and may even experience similar levels of anger, they are more likely to suppress and internalize their anger, whereas men are more likely to externalize theirs.

There is a cost to repression. For many women it may be "lowered self-esteem, a sense of powerlessness and fear of responding to or of even recognizing a provoking or unfair condition that causes the anger in the first place."[1]

Patty had gone through most of her life letting everyone else make her important decisions for her. She was most comfortable following the directions of others. She had learned that being a good wife and mother meant taking care of everyone else. She felt hopeless, helpless, inhibited and powerless. Yet at the same time she felt guilty for feeling that way.

Somewhere along the road she had learned that she wasn't important. God's promises really applied to everyone else. Patty feared rejection, criticism, disapproval or making a mistake. Since she was unaware of her emotions and couldn't face her own problems she became more vulnerable to experiencing physical problems.

By now you may have picked up the fact that the main characteristic of the cream puff is passivity. Cream puffs avoid making clear statements about what they think and feel, especially when their opinion might make someone else uncomfortable. Their energy is focused on protecting others and maintaining harmonious relationships.

Other characteristics of the typical cream puff include:

Anger suppressed	Denial	Responsible for
Anger turned inward	Dependent	others
Apathetic	Guilt-prone	Self-condemnation
Avoids problems	Overcontrolled	Self-pity
Conflict avoider	Passive reactor	Toxic shame

Cream puffs often fail to share their own legitimate needs and concerns and thus those around them are unaware of their pain. Over time they become less and less aware of their own feelings, thoughts and needs. They characteristically avoid any direct experience or expression of anger. In situations that in healthy people would evoke appropriate expressions of anger and protest they are likely to remain silent. They are more likely to say "I'm sorry" rather than "I'm hurt," "I'm afraid," "I'm frustrated" or "I'm angry." They apologize unnecessarily.

At one point in our work together, Patty observed, "In 22 years of marriage, I can count on one hand the number of times I've heard Ben say 'I'm sorry.' I've told myself that, since he is a man it's hard for him to apologize and that it's unfair for me to expect him to." Yet Patty felt an apology was necessary and so she would apologize for him.

In the short-term it is simpler and safer to apologize for something you haven't done. Inappropriate apologies tend to smooth things over, calm the waters, restore peace and tranquility, and avoid further confrontation and conflict. But there are tremendous long-term consequences. Inappropriate apologies let the guilty party off the hook, reinforcing their immaturity, insensitivity and irresponsibility and desensitizing them to problem areas in their own life. Inappropriate apologies hinder the growth, understanding and maturity of those we love.

Cream puffs avoid conflict like the plague. This failure to address deep problems and the insistence on avoiding conflict can lead to several negative results. First of all, since we haven't done anything about the problem, it still remains. Not only does the problem remain, it usually gets worse. As the problem gets worse our pain and fear increase. We experience even more fear, hurt, frustration and anger.

As we allow those feelings to smolder inside, we feel an even greater sense of hopelessness and helplessness. Continuing to ignore the problem only decreases our sense of value and worth and increases our sense of powerlessness. It becomes easier to focus on the problem and fail to see the resources we have in Christ.

Finally, it's easy for the anger that early on could have been appropriately communicated to someone else to be inappropriately directed inward toward ourselves. What's the result? We become immobilized, overwhelmed with discouragement and depression, overrun with guilt and shame, and unable to do anything.

Pain and misery are inevitable when our ways of relating to others consist of giving in, giving up and going along; when we assume responsibility for other peoples happiness; when we pretend that everything is going great when we know that it isn't; when we are so focused on everyone else that we ignore God's promises, provision and plan for our own lives.

When I was a kid I loved having water fights. Squirt guns were OK, but it was especially fun when there was a long water hose close by. I would turn the water on full power, bend the hose, let the pressure build up and then, just at the right time, straighten the hose out and let the water fly. The longer the flow of water had been interrupted, the greater the pressure of the water and the more damage I could do.

On the surface, it looks as though the cream puff has been able to turn off her anger faucet. But underneath, she really hasn't. That's because although we can for block the flow a limited time and choose not to express it, the emotion is still there. When the pressure builds up enough, the anger will flood out. If we don't learn how to express our anger in healthy ways, it will eventually find a way to express itself, often in a way that is unhealthy and destructive.

Do cream puffs ever experience anger? Of course they do. However, when provoked, they will usually say nothing. Most people think of anger as something hot such as in seething rage or an erupting volcano. But the cream puff's anger is usually more subtle and cold. He or she is someone whose immediate and automatic response to even the slightest hint of anger is to suppress it.

What does it mean to suppress anger? To suppress something means to hold in, to put it down by force, to prevent the natural or normal expression or development of something. When I suppress my anger, I'm aware of it, but through a lot of practice I'm able to keep it down. Few people are even aware that I'm angry. If over a period of time I continue to suppress my anger, it is likely that my anger will become repressed. When I repress my anger, it is kept from consciousness and I'm no longer even aware of it. People who have anger they're not aware of almost always express it in ways that are destructive to themselves and others. They are almost powerless to deal with it because they aren't really aware of it and they can't identify its cause.

Cream puffs are like boats drifting aimlessly on the ocean with no motor, oars or sails. They are forced to go wherever the wind blows them. But they are not totally without hope. The God-given emotion of anger can be a source of propulsion to move them out of their doldrums and help them move in healthy and constructive directions.

Locomotives

The opposite of the cream puff is the locomotive. In fact, one of the reasons many cream puffs lock themselves in a prison of passivity is their fear that if they ever let themselves get in touch with their anger they will become like the locomotive. Look over the following list of characteristics to see how different she is from the cream puff:

Anger against others	Hostile	Rage
Blatant sarcasm	Loud	Shallow
Combative	Obnoxious	Suspicious
Critical	Overconcern for self	Underresponsible
Cruel teasing	Overly competitive	
Driven	Power hungry	
Has all the answers	Prone to violence	
Has few intimate friends	Punitive	
	Quick to blame	

A locomotive doesn't have much time for the feelings or opinions of others. She has a sharp tongue and can be quick to criticize, put down and humiliate others. On the outside she appears confident, but inside she is riddled with fears and insecurities.

Because she needs so much acceptance, it is difficult for her to compliment others. It gives them the attention that she believes she deserves and needs for herself. She needs to be right all of the time and when she errs it will be on the side of being tough and not tender.

Whereas the cream puff is a passive reactor who doesn't give adequate attention to legitimate personal needs, the locomotive is an aggressive reactor who doesn't give adequate attention to others' needs and rights. Whereas the anger of the cream puff is usually implosive, the anger of the locomotive is most often explosive. When a locomotive gets angry, everyone around her knows it and anyone within eyesight is at risk of being yelled at and blamed.

When provoked, the locomotive, who already has a full head of steam, is likely to attack, label, put down and humiliate others. They often communicate in ways that violate the dignity and rights of other people. In Philippians 2:3 we are exhorted to regard one another as more important than ourselves. In 1 Peter 4:15 we read, "If you suffer, it must not be for murder, theft or sorcery, nor for infringing on the rights of others" (*NIV*). The locomotive consistently ignores these biblical principles or twists them as a basis for blaming others for not esteeming *him or her* as most important.

People who make a habit of dumping their anger on others don't get less angry; they tend to get more angry more often. When we choose to deal with our anger by an aggressive reaction style, it is easy for the anger to turn into rage. It doesn't take much for us to reach the boiling point and become steaming mad and spew a verbal shower of acid rain.

> *Aggression is usually an act of desperation—an attempt to overcome a sense of frustration and powerlessness.*

Many locomotive come from homes in which they suffered parental rejection, hostility and rage. There were no models of healthy anger. What they learned is that aggression can be an effective way to keep people at a distance so they can't hurt you and a way to pay back those who have hurt you. If you can get past the rough exterior of a locomotive, however, you will almost always find a good deal of hurt and fear.

Aggression is usually an act of desperation. It is often an attempt to overcome a sense of frustration and powerlessness. Although aggression may give us a sense of immediate satisfaction or relief, it doesn't last long. When we react in ways that are antagonistic, we are likely to breed even more antagonism. Negativity produces negativity. Attack increases the probability of counterattack. Attempts to coerce, overpower or trample only push others away and widens the gap between you.

Is there any hope for the locomotive? Susan Jacoby shares an encouraging story that says the answer is yes:

> I was always apologizing to someone for words spoken in the heat of anger. I exploded at people I loved and those I disliked, at family, friends, strangers, professional peers and even my bosses.
>
> Then, when I was 23, an incident at work literally changed my life. I was attached to a team of investigative reporters, and our boss was transferred to another department of the newspaper. We knew that Bob, a man we all liked very much, had been asked to replace him, and we were extremely disappointed when Bob turned down the job. Then an older editor called me into his office and explained that I—and my reputation for responding furiously to any criticism—was the problem.
>
> "Bob told me he just didn't want to put himself in a situation in which every little professional dispute would blow up into a big fight," the editor explained. Then he said something that hurt enormously at the time but turned out to be the biggest favor anyone has ever done me. "You know," he said, "you're very talented. If you weren't you would have been fired long ago, because it's so hard to work with you. You can't take criticism without blowing up, even if the criticism is justified. And if the criticism is not justified, you have no idea of how to bring other people around to your way of thinking without screaming and insulting them. Your anger is going to do you in if you don't learn how to express it differently."
>
> I was wounded and humiliated and—for once—had nothing to say. I usually forgot my outbursts as soon as they were over, and it was a revelation to learn that other people didn't forget so easily.

This realization was the beginning of a lifelong effort to control my anger—to separate the trivial from the genuinely important and to express truly legitimate anger in ways that were destructive neither to myself nor to others. At age 39, I still haven't succeeded entirely—but I have come a long way.[2]

When it comes to identifying their unhealthy anger style the majority of people would put themselves in the Cream Puff or Locomotive category. However there is a third anger style that in some ways is more subtle and complicated than the first two but just as unhealthy.

Steel Magnolias

The term "passive-aggressive" was first coined during World War II to describe the behaviors of certain soldiers. Because the military is highly structured for uniformity and compliance and individuality is not encouraged, the soldiers who didn't thrive under this kind of environment were observed to deal with it by resisting, ignoring orders, withdrawing or simply wanting out.

When you meet one of these "steel magnolias," what you see first is rarely what you'll end up getting. On the outside, you will see the lovely and sweet-smelling magnolia blossom. But more than just a casual encounter will reveal hardened steel. She is a contradiction to herself and to others. She is the master of the end-run. A part of you wants to trust her but the other part of you says that she can't be trusted.

You can trust the cream puff to yield to the desires and expectations of others in order to gain approval. You can trust the locomotive to ignore other people's desires and expectations. They are both fairly consistent. But you don't dare trust the steel magnolia. She may appear to be sensitive to the desires and expectations of others, but she'll often go ahead and do whatever she wants. She may appear to be passive but is actually quite aggressive.

The steel magnolia may appear calm, cool and collected on the outside, but just below the surface a huge cauldron of bitterness and resentment is boiling. At the core of every passive-aggressive person is an anger that hasn't been dealt with. It can be denied, disguised, suppressed, submerged or merely called something else. But that anger is never entirely concealed.

The steel magnolia doesn't state her needs; she is indirect. If you cross her or get in her way, you are in serious trouble. She may appear to be sensitive and tender on the outside, but don't get too comfortable because the tough side is sneaking up behind you.

Sarcasm is one of the most effective tools of the steel magnolia. She uses it to express anger while playing it safe. It is a way of attacking while avoiding a clearly hostile intent. Over time, individuals who use this tactic may convince themselves that they don't have aggressive feelings.

Using sarcasm, steel magnolias will disguise their anger with a smile and a joke. You know what I mean—the sarcastic, not-so-funny joke that makes you cringe rather than laugh, the funny comment that carries a subtle barb. It gets the message across, but it discourages retaliation because it doesn't leave you with many options. If you confront the steel magnolia, she will deny being angry. If you respond to the sarcasm, you may be accused of being negative, assuming the worst or not having a sense of humor.

Learn to recognize what's going on when you're dealing with a steel magnolia. If time after time you feel like you are receiving a double message, you probably are. Don't ignore your discomfort, feelings of frustration and confusion. If you don't feel listened to or cared about, you probably aren't. If you consistently feel put down rather than constructively criticized, that is probably the real intent. If a personal joke hurts, this could be an indicator that it was indeed meant to be a hostile barb rather than harmless fun.

Here are some characteristics of the steel magnolias. Notice how many of them express quiet rebellion.

Ambiguity	Inconsistency	Procrastination
Carelessness	Lies	Resentful
Chronic lateness	Makes excuses	Silent treatment
Fear of intimacy	Misunderstanding	Stubbornness
Forgetfulness	Mixed messages	Subtle sarcasm
Fosters confusion	Obstructionism	Sulking

No researcher has compared the number of male versus female steel magnolias, but it seems likely that many women prefer this style of anger. Raymond DiGiuseppe conducted a survey of 1,300 people ages 18 to 90 in which "women . . . were found to be angry longer, more resentful and less likely to express their anger, compared with men. . . . Women used indirect aggression by 'writing off' a higher number of people, intending never to speak to them again because of their anger."[3]

Where Do We Go From Here?

One of the main reasons these three anger styles are unhealthy and don't work is that they involve a denial of our real self. When we stuff, repress, suppress, deny, ignore or hurl our anger, we are ignoring anger's potentially important message. We have lost touch with the primary emotion that triggered our anger.

> *Resentment and rage keep reactors from dealing with legitimate fears and hurts and limit God's ability to bring recovery and restoration.*

Reactors deny their real grief and pain. Resentment and rage keep them from dealing with legitimate fears and hurts and limit God's ability to bring recovery and restoration. If we refuse to allow God to help us face the real issues of our lives, how can we understand, how can we forgive ourselves, how can we forgive others, how can we grow?

All three of the anger styles we have discussed thus far involve unhealthy reactions. They are usually an automatic and unconscious reaction to some real or perceived threat to our sense of significance, safety or security. Each style is dysfunctional. Each one falls short of God's plan and purpose in giving us the gift of anger. Fortunately God has given us a healthy option.

God can help you trade in your unhealthy reactive style for a mature, healthy and biblically sound way of understanding and expressing your anger.

The Mature (or Assertive) Responder

This healthy option is not an automatic *reaction* but involves a reasoned *response*. It is a way of responding that allows us to "Be angry and sin not." It is the assertive response.

Unfortunately the word "assertive" is often confused with the word "aggressive." But there is an enormous difference between the two. Sonya Friedman has this to say:

> Assertion and aggression are not identical. Here's why: Assertion is like having the right of way at the wheel of a late-model Cadillac; aggression is like deliberately plowing into another car at a demolition derby. Aggression is hostile comments or jokes at another's expense; assertion means using humor to defuse a volatile situation diplomatically or to connect to another human being by a shared sense of comedy. Aggression is a disregard for the consequences of your actions; assertion involves taking responsibility. Assertion is freedom from the persistent aggravation of a recurrent problem; aggression re-creates the problems. Assertion is common courtesy; aggression means pushing others around in their own lives.[4]

The *mature responder* is an assertive woman who has a clear sense of who she is in Christ. Her emotions, mind and will work together and function in a balanced way. She can express her opinions but doesn't need to put others down. She delights in serving but isn't servile. She can be tough and tender. She isn't reactive, she is proactive.

Whereas the anger of the cream puff is characterized by resentment and the anger of the locomotive is characterized by rage, the anger of the *mature responder* can be characterized by indignation. How does indignation differ from rage and resentment? In his book on anger, Richard Walters provides a very helpful comparison of the effects of all three emotions: rage, resentment and indignation.

Rage seeks to do wrong, resentment seeks to hide wrong, indignation seeks to correct wrongs. Rage and resentment seek to destroy people, indignation seeks to destroy evil. Rage and resentment seek vengeance, indignation seeks justice. Rage is guided by selfishness, resentment is guided by cowardice, indignation is guided by mercy. Rage uses open warfare, resentment is a guerrilla fighter, indignation is an honest and fearless and forceful defender of truth. Rage defends itself, resentment defends the status quo, indignation defends the other person. Rage and resentment are forbidden by the Bible, indignation is required. . . .

Rage blows up bridges people need to reach each other, and resentment sends people scurrying behind barriers to hide from each other and to hurt each other indirectly. Indignation is constructive: it seeks to heal hurts and to bring people together. Its purpose is to rebuild the bridges and pull down the barriers, yet it is like rage and resentment in that the feelings of anger remain.[5]

Without the mature response style, this angry world of ours would be a much poorer place. What are some characteristics of a *mature responder*?

Anger communicated	Healthy shame	Proactive
Careful	I win/You win	Responds
Caring	Indignation	Responsible
Constructive	Interdependent	Trusting
Direct communication	Listens	Unselfish
Firm	Motivated by love	Warm

The *mature responder* is free to "speak the truth in love." The cream puff will often speak in love, yet due to her overconcern for others, she may not speak the whole truth. Because she fears hurting someone's feelings or making waves, they may say whatever will not provoke the other person. The locomotive is not usually concerned with what others think or feel, so she is more likely to speak the truth as she sees it. However, it is rarely done with love. She is much more likely to dump and run.

When provoked, the *mature responder* is less likely to immediately react without thinking but rather responds in a way that reflects some discipline and thought. She has learned the value of anger. She has learned to be aware of and choose her expressions of anger. She is more likely to have trained herself to think, act and feel more constructively. She expresses her thoughts, preferences and emotions directly to the other person in healthy ways that communicate a respect for the dignity and the rights of both herself and others. Her response is more likely to move her toward achieving both her personal goals and her relational goals.

Anger can be an invaluable tool in the hands of a responsible person. It is a force capable of being directed and used constructively.

Take Action

1. Which of these three styles reflects you the most? Cream puff, locomotive or steel magnolia?
2. Where did you learn this style?
3. How to you see this pattern at work in your life?
4. How do others respond to this style? Be specific.
5. What steps can you take to become more of a *mature responder*?

WHY DO WOMEN GET ANGRY?

Gary J. Oliver

Karen woke up exhausted and weary. She had been in bed for seven hours but had tossed and turned most of the night. Her legs and back still ached from helping her best friend move a week earlier.

She got out of the house a little later than usual and the freeway traffic was at a standstill due to an accident. She had an important presentation to make at 10:00 A.M. and had wanted to get to work early to have more time to prepare. She had worked at this accounting firm for several years. Karen was a hard worker who consistently earned excellent reviews. Yet other male employees with less experience and less time with the company continued to be promoted before her. She was hoping that this presentation would help her get a much-deserved promotion.

When she finally arrived at work her boss happened to walk by and, noticing she was late, reminded her of the important presentation she had to make and told her how disappointed he was that she hadn't come in earlier.

In the afternoon she received a call from her son's principal that he had been involved in a fight at school and that he would have to stay after school. That meant he would miss the bus and that she would have to pick him up before going home to prepare a dinner she hadn't had time to even think about. At 6:00 P.M., just as she was putting the food on the table, her husband called to tell her a meeting had gone longer than expected and that he would be an hour late.

Reread these first three paragraphs and put yourself in Karen's shoes. You've just hung up the phone after talking to your husband. What are you thinking? What are you feeling? What do you feel like saying to him? What do you feel like saying to the world? What would you like to do?

You're probably asking, "Well, what did Karen do? How did she react?" Up to this point Karen had, from her perspective, done a great job of "holding it in." "I thought I was doing an admirable job of ignoring my fears and frustrations," Karen said with a hint of pride. "But when Tom called that was the last straw!" With a pause she looked down, shook her head and in a subdued tone of voice said, "I lost it!"

Now each of us has our own way of "losing it." We can get quieter or louder, we can withdraw or we can attack, we can blame others or blame ourselves, we can throw words or throw objects. Karen reacted by getting louder. She verbally attacked her husband and then her son, she blamed the traffic, her boss, her son, her husband and then she blamed life. "How did you feel after getting all that stuff out of your system?" I asked. "Did it accomplish anything positive?"

"I wish it had," she replied. "To be quite honest it felt great while I was dumping. But after it was over and especially after seeing the look on my son's face, I felt even worse than I did before I let it fly."

Can you remember a day in your life when it seemed as though nothing went right, when you encountered back-to-back pressures, demands, discouragements and criticism? By the end of the day what were some of your thoughts? Can you recall some of the emotions you felt? When the "last straw" hit what was your immediate response? How do you wish you had responded? Do you remember why you were angry?

Why was Karen angry? Was it the achy body from helping her friend move, the lousy night's sleep, leaving home later than she had expected, the traffic jam, the pressure of her presentation, her boss's critical remark, frustration with the gender bias at work, her son's getting in trouble, having to change her schedule to pick him up, having to prepare dinner while being exhausted after a draining day, her husband's phone call—or was it a combination of all of these?

One of the things that makes anger a difficult emotion to deal with is that when we experience anger there is rarely only one source or "cause." From our research and from our own experience it's obvious that there are any number of situations that can trigger an anger response.

In our book *When Anger Hits Home*, we identified the 10 major causes of anger in men and women. These were: childhood experiences, physiological factors, accumulated stress from normal everyday events, injustice, low self-esteem, worry, conflict, fear, hurt and frustration.[1] In 1993, Sandra Thomas conducted the Women's Anger Study, a large-scale investigation involving 535 women between the ages of 25 and 66. The study revealed three common roots to women's anger: powerlessness, injustice and the irresponsibility of other people.[2]

At anger workshops and in our interviews and surveys we have asked women, What are some of the specific factors that increase your vulnerability to getting angry? What situations or circumstances make it more likely for you to experience anger? In a group of close to 100 women, we received over 200 different responses. Some of the most frequently mentioned responses include the following:

Abandonment

Being a people-pleaser

Dealing with children

Discrimination because I'm a
    woman

Disrespect

Entitlement of men

Feeling insecure around people

Feeling sorry for myself

Getting older

Having to wait

Lack of affection from spouse

Not dealing with previous anger

Not enough quiet time for
    myself

Not having my feelings valued

Overcommitment

PMS

People talking behind my back

Selfish demands

Stress

Teenagers and in-laws

Tired and worn out

Unfair comparison

Unrealistic expectations

When I see I've gained weight

When I sin

When I'm not taken care of

When I've been embarrassed or
 laughed at

When I've been used or betrayed

When we looked at all of the factors listed by the women, we were able to identify several factors that can contribute to or are likely to trigger an anger response. Notice I said *contribute to* rather than *cause*. That is an important distinction. The exact same event can occur to five different people and there can be five different emotional reactions. There are a number of situations that can increase the probability that a person will experience anger.

But as you already know, anger itself isn't the main problem. It is only a symptom. The real problem is our difficulty we have in identifying and understanding our anger and thereby choosing healthy ways to express it. The first step in anger management is to identify and understand the root causes of our anger. Without this it will be almost impossible to make our anger work for us.

> *The first step in anger management is to identify and understand the root causes of our anger.*

Double Standard

Why do women get angry? Women get angry for many of the same general reasons that men get angry: injuries, attacks, injustice, intrusions, disappointments, threats, innuendos, misunderstandings, fear, hurt and frustration. However, while men and women's anger often have similar causes, social and cultural conditions have contributed in a unique way to women's anger. In addition, studies have found that women's anger is more likely to result from another person's actions within a close relationship, whereas men are more likely to be angered by the actions of strangers.[3]

Few people would debate the fact that for many years women have been discriminated against. Why? Merely for being women. This sometimes subtle and at other times blatant discrimination has created a more hostile environment for women. It puts them in situations in which they have more reasons to be afraid, are more likely to be hurt and are more likely to experience frustration. All of these emotions can be root causes of and lead to the emotion of anger. This double standard creates an environment in which it is more likely that women will experience anger.

The double standard of our culture displays itself in many ways. We are quick to view a woman who expresses anger as a sick, troubled, disturbed or irrational persona. Men have "clear convictions," but women are "opinionated." A man is described as "an assertive and strong leader" while a woman with the same qualities is called "strong-willed." A woman's healthy expression of anger, criticalness or competitiveness directed toward a man is often interpreted as an unhealthy display of aggression or an attempt to control. I've heard terms like "hostile," "domineering" or "controlling" used to describe a woman's expression of anger when a similar expression by the man was termed "strong" or "confident." In the face of such a double standard, a woman's main options are to stuff, repress, suppress or deny the emotion of anger, and that, of course, will only decrease her sense of value and worth and increase her sense of powerlessness.

Women are born into a socially subordinate position and, according to Jean Baker Miller, a professor of psychiatry at the Boston University School of Medicine, simply being born into a subordinate position can generate anger. The dominant group doesn't allow the expression of that anger so it gets repressed. Eventually it can develop into a much larger sense of undirected rage. Because that feeling of anger and frustration is sometimes falsely referred to as a "bottomless well," many women may be afraid to tap into it.[4]

A recent poll indicated that the second-most-mentioned complaint of women is that they are frustrated with the division of the workload at home. Women work an average of 15 hours more than men per week—including household chores. By any standard this isn't fair and it is a major source of resentment in many women. One woman told me, "I wasn't even aware of it at first. I just thought that's the way it is. That's what women do. But after 10 years I started resenting Bob. I became more negative and critical and I wasn't sure why."

It took her close to a year to realize that the real source of her frustration and anger wasn't because her husband was a bad person. It was because of the unidentified and unacknowledged hurt and resentment that had accumulated over years of living under this double standard.

Another study found that 39 percent of women—as compared to 26 percent of men—mentioned "neglect of home or children" as a major cause of divorce. It was the second-most-common reason that women cited for divorce—behind "mental cruelty" but ahead of financial problems, physical abuse, drinking or even infidelity.[5]

Unrewarding Work

In my counseling I have observed that another major source of anger in our contemporary life is the unrewarding work that many people are engaged in. Today many people are engaged in work where they play an intermediary role. They know what they do is dispensable. Their work is a series of intermediate and repetitive tasks whose fruits are rarely evident. Very few workers today have a part in the end-result of their work with which they can identify and feel pride over.

Whatever diminishes our sense of value, worth and significance increases our sense of powerlessness. This can either increase our desire for approval and thus increase our vulnerability to being taken advantage of. Or it can contribute to a spirit of "I could care less" in which people give up trying or respond by attacking the system.

According to our interviews and survey this principle is especially applicable in the lives of some mothers and homemakers. Many women have expressed that being a homemaker is a lonely and often thankless role. Many women feel they are victims of a double-edged sword. If they stay at home they feel unappreciated and unrewarded. If they go out of the home into the workplace, they face bias and discrimination.

Connie is a friend of our family and has a delightful sense of humor. In a recent conversation she captured well the frustration that many women feel. She shared that in the past week her husband Bob came home and excitedly talked about the major deal he had closed and the fact that he would probably get a $5,000 bonus. He was especially excited that his boss made a point of congratulating him in front of other senior management.

Now on the one hand I was truly delighted for him and for the family. He has worked long and hard on this contract and we can use the money. But on the other hand it frustrates and angers me. When he comes home what do I have to share with him? That I cleaned the house and picked up our two preschoolers' toys seven times, that I changed 11 damp and soiled diapers and prepared a meal that will be downed in 15 minutes to be followed by the joy of dishes? And then when the kids are in bed I can anticipate another thrilling day of doing exactly the same thing. Well, not exactly the same. The number of dirty diapers can vary.

Where's my compliment and what's my bonus? Can't you just see Bob coming up to me saying, "Honey, I want you to know that you really have a gift with baby wipes. I know other women who would take at least two or three of them to clean up what you are able to clean up with just one. I sure don't deserve a gifted hard-working wife like you. I can't tell you how much it means for me to know that our babies bottoms are in such good hands."

Now in fairness to Connie, she loves being able to be a full-time mom. She doesn't have to be. She chose to be. Both she and Bob share the belief that what she is doing is, in the long run, a significant investment of her life and their resources. On several occasions I've heard Bob say (and I know that he means it) that what Connie does is much more important and valuable than what he does.

Yet at the same time it is clearly more routine, more mundane, less challenging, less stimulating and less rewarding in the sense of short-term, tangible rewards. "I can tell myself that it doesn't matter, that it shouldn't matter, that if I was a bit more spiritual it wouldn't matter," Connie stated. "But the reality is that sometimes it does matter."

Shame

These cultural conditions and social demands make many women especially vulnerable to the ravages of unhealthy shame. One woman wrote,
"I think my parents should have named me Avis because I have lived my
life believing that I've always got to try harder." Her humor served as a
thin veil to much deeper layers of guilt and shame.

God designed the emotion of shame to lead us to Himself. Healthy
shame says, "God loves me. I have been made in His image. I have value
and worth. But I am also a sinner. I am not perfect. I have made and will
make mistakes. I need God." Healthy shame leads us to acknowledge
both the fact that we are image-bearers as
well as the reality of our sinful humanity
and that reality drives us to the Cross.

When shame becomes the basis for
our identity, the shame that God intended
for good can become unhealthy. A shame-
based person is one who focuses on her
shame to the exclusion of Christ's completed work for her on the cross. At this
point shame becomes toxic and hazardous
to our emotional and spiritual health.

Women who are shame-based either
ignore or are functionally unaware of the
reality of who they are in Christ and of
what He accomplished in their behalf at
the cross. They are unaware of their legitimate needs as well as God's promise and
plan for their life. They have little sense of their value and worth, have
given up on the possibility of experiencing the abundant life and because
of the undercurrent of hopelessness and helplessness, they often aban-
don their opportunities to grow and to become all that God would have
them to be.

At first they ignore and then they eventually become numb to their
own feelings and needs. Like Connie they tell themselves that what they

> *Healthy shame says, "God loves me. I have been made in His image. But I am also a sinner. I have made and will make mistakes. I need God."*

feel doesn't matter, isn't valid, isn't important, is a sign of developmental or spiritual immaturity, or is just plain sinful.

They set aside appropriate personal goals to achieve the relational goal of harmony. After all, aren't women supposed to be the great peacemakers? The price for peace is often their own God-given uniqueness, individuality and identity. While ignoring their own happiness they are more vulnerable to assume responsibility for the happiness of others. At times they will even go so far as to take the blame for something they haven't even done.

Their unhealthy shame leads them down the primrose path of perfectionism and into the welcoming arms of a performance-based life. This is the kind of life where your value and worth is determined by what you do and how well you do it rather than who you are or, to put it more succinctly, who God has declared that you are.

Over time this unrewarding and unfulfilling lifestyle leads to an attempt to numb the pain of meaninglessness through increased busyness, even higher standards, greater guilt and shame or the adrenaline rush we get from "losing our temper." We become more negative and critical of others because it is always easier to focus on the faults and weaknesses of others. If my focus is on what is wrong with everyone else I don't have time to be aware of my own stuff.

David Seamands has written,

> I have yet to counsel a performance-based and perfectionistic Christian who was not at heart an angry person. This doesn't mean such persons are always aware of or express it openly. They often impress us as being extremely controlled or very loving. But when we get to know them better, and they open up to share their inner selves, we inevitably discover a core of anger deep within their personalities.[6]

Hurt

Hurt is one of those emotions that we all experience but don't like to talk about. In fact when we talk about the hurt we often relive the experience, reexperience the pain and can become retraumatized. Over time it's easy for hurt to turn into boiling resentment.

Hurt is another one of those uncomfortable emotions that can often lead to anger. Where there is anger there is almost always some kind of pain. Where there is pain something is usually broken and needs to be fixed.

When we're hurt we are vulnerable, weak, drained, hopeless and helpless. When the pain of hurt is denied and stuffed into the unconscious we may not think about it but that doesn't mean it has magically disappeared. Out of mind does not mean out of memory.

Anger puts up a wall to protect us from hurt. The short-term effect is that we don't hurt. The long-term effect is that the problems we have been avoiding and trying to run from get worse and the hurt is always greater than it would have been if we had used our anger-energy to address the problem in the first place.

Where there is anger there is almost always some kind of pain. Where there is pain something is usually broken and needs to be fixed.

Eventually the layers of hurt, confusion and misunderstanding make it more difficult to access the facts and interpretations that caused it. Unfortunately the pain of repressed hurt can simmer for years. Like smoke rising out of the campfire anger can rise up out of the embers of hurt. If not dealt with, it can suddenly boil to the surface moving past the potentially positive emotion of anger to the damaging emotion of rage.

Hurt is emotionally draining, and anger can give us the energy required to throw up walls to protect ourselves. At first the walls can keep people out and thus keep the hurt out. Anger can veil the hurt, fear, pain and sense of loss that comes from real or perceived rejection. *If no one gets close to me, then no one can hurt me,* we think.

Many people are surprised to learn that hurt and anger go hand in hand. It's not uncommon to assume that the angry person is so insensitive they must be incapable of being hurt. That's just the point. Frequently the obnoxious person is the one who has experienced deep hurt, often in their childhood. It's a fact that we are more likely to be hurt by people who are important to us. Therefore we are more likely to feel anger towards people who are important to us.

It's important to learn how to distinguish between hurt and anger. Dr. Paul Welter has written that for the most part hurt is the first emotion to be felt but the one that is least accessible to memory. Anger is the second emotion we experience and the one we are most aware of.[7] If we ignore the warning sign of our anger, it can easily turn into resentment and a desire for revenge. If we allow it to have its way, resentment will keep us imprisoned in our past, it will poison our present and ravage our future.

Frustration

There are numerous sources of frustration in a woman's life. The majority of frustrations fall under the categories of blocked goals and desires or unmet needs and expectations. Frustrations are those seeming little things that, if they happen with enough frequency or at the wrong time, can become big things.

For example, you have just spent close to an hour scrubbing and cleaning the tile floors. Suddenly, one of your children opens the patio door, and in rushes your dog, who has been digging out in the snow-covered yard. In a matter of seconds not only does your tile floor look a mess but in trying to catch your dog he (it must be a he because a female dog would be more sensitive) runs through the living room and now it is a mess too. Your children were trying to help and your dog thought everyone wanted to play with him, but now you have twice as much work to do. At this moment what is your view of dogs, children, housework and your source of meaning and purpose in life? What are some of the emotions you are feeling? What did you have to keep yourself from saying? How loud would your voice have been if you had said?

You are late for an appointment, but finally the traffic in the lane next to you seems to be moving. You put your turn signal on, change lanes and are starting to make good time. You breathe a sigh of relief and say to yourself "If this keeps up, I won't be late after all." Suddenly a car pulls in front of you going 10 miles an hour slower than the rest of traffic. What are you thinking now? What are you feeling? What would you like to say to that driver?

But the frustration so many women feel doesn't come only from the myriad ordinary things that happen to us on a daily basis. The women in our research indicated they are frustrated with not being appreciated for what they do; by feeling like they are not good enough as a wife/mother/daughter/friend/career person; by excessive demands and unreal expectations; by feelings of powerlessness; and "by being expected to look like the women in magazines and on billboards who work part-time, have personal fitness trainers, have had surgeons work on their face, legs and other body parts, have people who cook their meals and clean their homes."

An increasing number of women are frustrated by their need to choose between wanting to be a full-time vocational mom and yet having to work outside the home.

Cindy lives with this frustration. A 38-year-year-old mother of 3, she works at a factory where her shift can run 12 hours a day during the busy summer season. "I never feel like I'm a full-time mom," she said. "I bake cookies, make lunches and homemade costumes for Halloween. I volunteer for everything I can to make up to them for not being there. By the time I do all of that, I'm so worn out that my kids end up with an exhausted and crabby mom. I'm frustrated and discouraged by the fact that no matter what I do it's never enough." It's not that there aren't any solutions to these frustrations. It's just that most of the time those solutions don't come easily.

Another source of frustration that is coming to the surface is the gender bias that we discussed earlier in this chapter. For example, many women believe that there is a "glass ceiling" that blocks their ability to rise to the upper levels of the corporate world. They face unequal access to credit, exclusion from government contracts and, at times, blatant discrimination. It's not fair and that's frustrating.

Women are frustrated with being told that they are not strong enough, not smart enough, not tough enough, not fast enough, not this or that enough. The good news is that as we identify the role of anger in our lives in light of what the Bible says about this important emotion, the hurt and frustration can be turned into healing and hope. Before going on to the next chapter, it will be valuable for you to work through the Take Action section.

Take Action

Some Questions Regarding Hurt

- When was the last time you experienced a significant hurt?
- How and when were you hurt? Who hurt you?
- Have you ever experienced a similar kind of hurt in the past?
- How did you deal with it then? What did you learn from it?
- Is there any way you could have prevented the hurt?
- If so, how? Why didn't you? If not, why not?
- What part of you experienced the injury? Your sense of self-worth? Your trust? Your pride? Your competence?
- Could you be hanging on to your hurt as a way to control others?
- Does holding on to a grudge justify your staying angry?

How to Identify Your Anger Pattern

For the next 30 days maintain an Anger Log. Whenever you become aware of anger, grab your Anger Log and record the following information:

- The date and time of day.
- Rate the intensity of your anger from 1 to 10, with 1 meaning the anger is barely noticeable, and a 10 meaning that you have gone beyond anger into rage. (In fact a 10 means that you were totally out of control.)
- Where possible, identify the primary emotion or emotions that led to the secondary emotion of anger.

- What is the issue that led to your anger? (You will not always be able to identify the issue.)
- How do you talk to yourself about the situation? Does your self-talk reflect passive or aggressive reactions or an assertive response?

Here is a sample for an entry into the Anger Log:

Date _____   Time _____

Intensity: 1   2   3   4   5   6   7   8   9   10

Primary Emotion: (a) Hurt   (b) Frustration   (c) Fear   (d) Other

Issue:

Self-Talk:

CHAPTER 7

STRESS, FATIGUE AND ANGER

H. Norman Wright

Take a moment to reflect on the following questions:

- Do you ever find yourself struggling with making decisions? Not only the major ones but the little ones as well?
- Are fleeting thoughts becoming more common, thoughts such as, *Oh, I'd like to get away from all of this. I want to get away from my kids, my husband, my job—everything. I need a break!*
- Do you find yourself increasing your use of stimulants to keep you going—alcohol, cigarettes, coffee, Cokes, tranquilizers or diet pills? Do you find your mind taking a vacation on you, finding your thoughts trailing off when you are speaking to someone or writing?
- Do you worry excessively? You know what worry is. You go over and over a real or imagined situation in your mind. You begin to take on the worries of others as well as your own.
- Do you find yourself snapping and exploding at others because your anger is riding just under the surface, and it doesn't take much for it to explode?

- Are you finding it difficult to trust others? Is your suspicion index starting to climb even with close friends and family members?
- Are you beginning to forget appointments, dates and deadlines? Do you find yourself brooding over events and issues, even little ones?
- Are people beginning to say that you just don't seem quite yourself anymore?[1]

All of the items above are symptoms of stress overload. "Stress" is a simple, common word. It has been used as a catchall to explain a physical and emotional response when no other explanation can be found. But stress is real, and it's directly correlated to anger. Stress can generate anger, and anger can generate stress. In our national survey, stress was identified as the second leading factor that increases women's vulnerability to anger.

Defining Stress

What exactly is stress? It is any situation or condition that chronically irritates or upsets you. Because of it you are thrown out of balance physically and psychologically. Under stress you're the victim of a flood of adrenaline.

Stress is the feeling of being drawn tight like a rubber band when it is stretched taut and stays in that position. When the pressure is released, the rubber band returns to normal, but if it stays in that position too long, the rubber begins to lose its elastic qualities, becomes brittle, develops cracks and eventually breaks.

What is stressful to one woman is not to another. Your background, life experience, how you learned to handle the upsets of life, and your neurological structure will affect your response.

Not all stress is bad. Good stress can motivate and activate us, and it doesn't last long. It brings a feeling of exhilaration.

One woman therapist searched through a decade of therapy notes with her female clients and looked for distinctly female stress. She found—

- Stresses associated with physiology: breast development, menstruation, pregnancy and menopause.
- Stresses connected to life changes: becoming a wife or a mother, enduring a divorce or economic collapse, moving into the 40s in a youth-oriented society, having adult children return home and widowhood.
- Psychological stresses experienced by the lonely single woman and the homemaker coping with the pressure to go back to school or develop a career; or those experienced by the career woman who is pressured to give it up, go back home and be a stay-at-home mom; or those endured by the exhausted working woman who is constantly short on sleep and money.
- The not-so-apparent stressors that tend to not only distract a woman but over time also deplete her resources, leading to a feeling of distress. They include the pressure of commuting, being isolated with young children, the threat of being attacked because of being a woman, fighting chauvinism, sexist comments and harassment.
- The life crises that unfortunately tend to be handled more by women than by men. Those can include caring for a sick or dying parent or child, parenting a handicapped child and handling the aftermath of her own or her child's divorce.[2]

Stressed? Here's Why

Let's take a closer look at some of the reasons why you—or any woman today—might experience stress.

Barriers, Contradictory Feelings, Changing Expectations

In *Beyond Chaos: Stress Relief for the Working Woman*, Sheila West talks about "the glass ceiling" and what West calls "the reeling effect." The glass ceiling is a perceived barrier that allows women to glimpse, but prevents them from obtaining, positions further up the corporate ladder.

The reeling effect is difficult to overcome, since its ingredients are change plus apprehension, equaling uncertainty. Many women experience this. Constant change along with apprehension about their work leaves them feeling as though they just stepped out of a tornado.[3] It's the mixture of opposite feelings: "Oh, I really want to work" versus "When am I going to be able to quit?" and "Is it always going to be like this?" or "This is so challenging and informative" versus "How will I survive all these deadlines? Help!" Sheila West comments on the contradictory feelings that create the sense of uncertainty in women:

> The phrase "just a job" conjures up unpleasant associations: mundane assignments, boring routines, something to be endured. In this kind of environment, our feelings are bound to fluctuate with daily activities in an aimless moodiness. . . . And [if] we receive a meager paycheck to boot, we'll continue to question whether we made the right choice. . . . Even women on a career track are often caught off guard with what they find in the marketplace. There doesn't seem to be much security or continuity in many fields.
>
> Women often find that staying on the competitive edge means treacherous climbing rather than sustaining accomplishments. The thrill of a new challenge gives way to the agony of moving too fast to be adequately prepared. We thought we knew what we wanted, but once we get it we're not sure it's what we had in mind.
>
> The reeling effect keeps us frustrated over the constant effort to prove ourselves, the energy required to avoid unnecessary confrontations with others, and the enduring stress of having to maintain high-quality performance. The stress can reach the point where even if we do love work, we want out anyway. The pleasure of accomplishment is just not worth the struggle for survival.[4]

Single in a Married World

Today's woman is more likely to experience a divorce. More than half of today's married women will end up divorced. More women than before will never marry, and more of those who do won't ever have a child.

Nevertheless, if you're single you'll experience stress because of it, especially if you're getting older and want to get married. If you're over 34, you have a problem, as the pool of eligible men is very small. The stress of "I must find a man" that propels many women in their 30s and 40s keeps them from living a full life. There is another stress as well. How does our society view single women? Is it a positive or negative view? The stereotype is that single women are unhappy and perhaps defective in some way.[5]

New Freedoms, Fewer Options

What generates so much stress and anger is that few women end up having the life they thought they were going to get when they were growing up. Yes, there are new freedoms and changes, but there are also fewer options. A permanent marriage, children and handling work and home are not sure things. What accompanies the new options and lifestyle is enormous stress, much more than ever before.

> *What generates so much stress and anger is that few women end up having the life they thought they were going to get when they were growing up.*

The doors have opened for more work for women, but that has added much more stress to women's lives. Working wives and mothers have discovered that they are still expected to run the home and fulfill the same duties they did when they were just at home and the cost of day care impacts them. Husbands do not help out that much, partly because they are let off the hook too easily. Naturally, that causes stress and anger and eventually resentment.

Guilt over Working

Many working wives, and especially mothers struggle with guilt over working. To make up for it, they put forth a double effort at home to show that they are adequate mothers and can handle both work and homemaking. Soon they're stressed; running on an empty tank, and candidates for burnout.[6]

Too much to do, too little time. Even when they have financial problems, two out of three women say they would prefer more time rather than money.[7]

Many women tend to add pressure to their life by taking on too much or attempting to accomplish too much in a limited time span. Often they continually take on new activities, never evaluating which ones are really important and therefore never dropping any. Time-pressured women may be driven by their own unrealistic ideals, by the expectations of others, or both.

Fatigue

As stated in an earlier chapter, women identified fatigue as the number one contributor for making them vulnerable to anger. Fatigue is also one of the main contributors to depression—and to stress. Many women, single and married, begin to feel worn down as they try to juggle having a career with the other demands in their lives.

Insufficient sleep is also a major factor here. Mounting evidence points to sleep deprivation as one of the major problems in our country.[8] The majority of women do not get the seven to eight hours of sleep a night that sleep experts tell us we need in order to function at our best. They only average five to six hours a night—an insufficient amount, which over time will erode a person's resources. Too little sleep results in less emotional control, less energy, less clear thinking and a greater tendency to be at risk for illness, accidents, conflict and anger.[9]

Boredom

Boredom—or lack of meaning in what you do—can cause stress. This may come as a surprise to you but it's true: continually doing the same routine or being bored can become a stressor. Homemakers and those in routine jobs may struggle with this. Sometimes a woman may have to work at discovering the meaning in what she is involved in doing. She may need to become creative and develop some new ways of responding to a monotonous environment.

Unrealistic Expectations

Unrealistic expectations will keep you stressed. We all have expectations for ourselves and for others. But can they all be attained? Where did they come from? Perfectionists are people with excessively unobtainable expectations. They are great candidates for stress. There is a difference between living a life of perfectionism (or attempting to, since no one has ever been successful at it yet), and a life of excellence. *Webster's Dictionary* states that to be "perfect" is to be "complete and flawless in all respects."[10]

If you are in a job ill-suited to you, it may be stressful. Feeling stuck will build your anger.

"Excellence" is defined as something "outstandingly good or exceptional merit."[11] Perfection is defined by absolutes. Excellence, on the other hand, means you do things to the best of your ability, and you make mistakes.

Perfection is an end state, whereas excellence allows for forgiveness. A perfectionist may be 98 percent successful in something but allows the 2 percent to white out all the success. She focuses on the flaw and doesn't see the value in progress. Remember that if you are striving to be a perfectionist, you are still living by works and have not yet learned to live by the grace of God.

Role Conflicts

If you are in a job ill-suited to you, it may be stressful. If you are a housewife and would rather be following a career, you may experience stress. Feeling stuck will build your anger.

Communication Blocks

If you are dating or married and open communication is blocked, stress will build. Relationships are built upon communication. When a spouse or parent refuses to talk or puts pressure on others to be quiet, there will be damaging results. In a marriage relationship, when one partner is either overly quiet or pulls the silent treatment, very little intimacy can develop.

This is one of the major causes of marital disruption and destruction.

Pressures of the Workplace

The '90s ushered in what is referred to as "the era of the new woman." Many more women work than ever before. It is estimated that 99 percent of the women in this country have worked or will work for pay at some time during their lives. Most women work because they have to, but many have said they would work even if they didn't have to. They've assessed the benefits of being employed. Many more women today see their work as a career rather than just a job, which means they have a greater personal investment in it.

The jobs that women hold today are more of the stressful, pressure-laden ones. In 1988 women made up 39 percent of all those holding managerial, executive and administrative positions—a 13 percent jump from 10 years before.

Women have discovered that work not only brings in money but can also generate stress. Sometimes the stress overrides the benefits. Many factors contribute to that stress:

- having a great deal of responsibility, but little authority or control;
- having an abundance of work, but insufficient time to complete it;
- having a strong desire to advance in your job, but the chances are limited;
- discovering you are more competent than your boss, but are still being ignored;
- being underpaid for what you do, or discovering that men in the same position are paid more;
- having a lot to do, but constantly being interrupted;
- doing work that is not exciting, challenging or stimulating, but is instead boring and redundant;
- experiencing sexual harassment or discrimination on the job;
- holding a clerical job (where the above factors are experienced most frequently).[12]

"Type A" Syndrome

As described by cardiologists Meyer Friedman and Ray Rosenman, the "Type A" syndrome used to be a condition of achievement-oriented males. But we now recognize this condition in women with high-pressure jobs. The most dangerous factors connected with this problem are time urgency and chronic anger. Much of the anger stems from insufficient time and too much to do, unrealistic expectations and guilt.

Type A women experience *free-floating hostility*, a sense of lasting, indwelling anger. This hostility increases in frequency, demonstrating itself even in the most minor frustrations. Type A women may be clever at hiding this tendency or finding excuses and reasons for their irritation. But they become upset too frequently, and in a way that is out of proportion. They are overly and outwardly critical, and they belittle and demean others.

Time urgency manifests itself in two ways. First, the Type A woman speeds up her activities. The way she thinks, plans and carries out tasks is accelerated. She talks faster and forces others to do the same. It is difficult to relax around her. Everything must be done faster, and she looks for ways to increase the speed. Second, she has many different thoughts and activities on the burner at the same time. Leisure time doesn't reduce the tension, for she overschedules activities even then. She attempts to find more time and tries to do two or three things at once. She overextends herself in a multitude of activities and projects, and often some go undone.

In time your body will tell you if your behavior is Type A. A true Type A person's body experiences more adrenaline, a hormone which constricts the blood vessels and pushes up blood pressure.

Cumulative Stress

In the 1970s two medical doctors named T. H. Holmes and R. H. Rahe developed the Holmes-Rahe stress test, which has been widely used and then revised for women. The Holmes-Rahe test is based upon a series of life events, with each event receiving a numerical score for its stress potential or value. In the original sample the researchers discovered that those with scores over 300 points for the past year had an 80 percent chance of experiencing an illness or depression within the next two years, because of the amount of stress they were experiencing. The results showed the correlation between life change stress and physical and emotional stress.

In the updated survey 2,300 women in 20 states were surveyed to see how they were affected by the same events listed in the original survey. The top 10 stressors are listed below. The numbers in parentheses are the point values for each.

Top 10 Stressors
1. Death of Spouse (99)
2. Divorce (91)
3. Marriage (85)
4. Death of close family member (89)
5. Fired at work (83)
6. Marital separation (78)
7. Pregnancy (78)
8. Jail term (72)
9. Death of a close friend (68)
10. Retirement (68)[13]

Those who participated in the revised survey were given the opportunity to add new stressors to the original list. The list below shows the top 13 items they mentioned, and also indicates the new point values for each item.

New Stressors
Disabled child (97)
Single parenting (96)
Remarriage (89)
Depression (89)
Abortion (89)
Infertility (87)

Child's illness (87)
Spouse's illness (85)
Crime victimization (84)
Husband's retirement (82)
Parenting parents (81)
Chemical dependency (80)
Raising teens (80)
Parent's illness (78) [14]

The changes in stress patterns are quite apparent. Where do you fit in all of this? Do you agree with the ratings of these stressors? What are the five major stressors in your life at the present time? What are the effects in your life because of each one? Which of these especially evokes or heightens your anger?

Stress That Has Reached the Burnout Stage

I've talked with many women who have said they used to feel they were stressed and were quite angry over their situation, but now they just don't have the energy to be angry. It's as though they don't care anymore. That isn't stress. It's burnout—and there are several varieties: overall burnout, parental burnout, job burnout, marital burnout.

A simple, overall definition of "burnout" is: "to wear oneself out by excessively striving to reach some unrealistic expectation imposed by one's self or by the values of society." Someone who is burned out is "in a state of fatigue or frustration brought about by devotion to a cause, way of life, or relationship that failed to produce the expected reward." Burnout produces a sense of helplessness and hopelessness.

Burnout is a complex process that involves all five major areas of our lives: physical, intellectual, emotional, social and spiritual. The physical aspect refers to the amount of energy available to do what you need to do and want to do. Burnout's first symptom is an all-around feeling of fatigue. The intellectual aspect refers to the sharpness with which you think and solve problems. In burnout, this ability diminishes. The emotional aspect refers to whether your emotional life is basically positive or negative—whether you are optimistic or pessimistic about what is occurring in your life. The social aspect of burnout refers to feelings of isolation, compared to feelings of involvement. What kind of support system do you have? Do you feel free to share your feelings of frustration, anger, fatigue or disillusionment? The spiritual aspect refers to the degree of meaning you have in your life.

Perhaps you're wondering whether you're simply stressed or have burnout. Consider the differences between the two:

- Burnout is a defense characterized by disengagement.
  Stress is characterized by overengagement.
- In burnout the emotions become blunted.
  In stress the emotions become overreactive.
- In burnout the emotional damage is primary.
  In stress the physical damage is primary.
- The exhaustion of burnout affects motivation and drive.
  The exhaustion of stress affects physical energy.
- Burnout produces demoralization.
  Stress produces disintegration.
- The depression of burnout is caused by the grief engendered
  by the loss of ideals and hope.
  The depression of stress is produced by the body's need to
  protect itself and conserve energy.

Overcoming Stress

How do you lessen the stress in your life and make yourself less prone to anger? You could try to change your environment, whether it be working conditions, home schedule, travel or moving. Some things, however, are difficult to change. Relaxation techniques do help. Tranquilizers are sometimes prescribed for stress, but it should be remembered that some people become overly dependent on tranquilizers.

Perhaps the best approach, after you have taken all the corrective action possible, is to change your thoughts and perspective on what is taking place in your life. At the heart of most of life's stress is your attitude—your belief system. If you are stuck on the freeway and have an appointment in 20 minutes for which you will now be late, what do you say to yourself? Do you sit there and make statements such as, "I can't be late! Who's holding us up? I've got to get out of this lane!"

> *But what moves you from feeling like a victim to becoming an overcomer is taking control of your circumstances by giving yourself permission to be in the situation you're in.*

Yes, it's inconvenient to be stuck, to be late, to have the boss pile on work at the last minute or to miss the bus. But what moves you from feeling like a victim to becoming an overcomer is taking control of your circumstances by giving yourself permission to be in the situation you're in: to have your plans disrupted or to be given too much work or whatever it may be. That will put you back in control, and you'll feel there is some hope.

It works. It's learning to put Philippians 4:13 into practice: "I can do all things through Christ who strengthens me" (*NKJV*). Proverbs 15:15 applies also: "All the days of the desponding and afflicted are made evil [by anxious thoughts and forebodings], but he who has a glad heart has a continual feat [regardless of circumstances]" (*AMP*).

Here are a number of suggestions for changing your responses and reducing the stress and fatigue in your life. Making these changes may be uncomfortable at first because you are giving up a way of life that is has become familiar. It may take a while to see a change and it will certainly take some effort—but it is worth it to reduce the stress in your life.

- Begin each day by asking God to help you prioritize those items that need to be done first. Then do only those items you really have time for. If you feel you can accomplish five items during the day, do only four. Write them down and then check them off.

- If you begin to feel pressured about completing your tasks, ask yourself these questions: *Will completing this task matter three to five years from now? Must it be done now? If so, why? Could someone else do it? If not, why not?*
- Try to accomplish only one thing at a time. If you are going to the bathroom, don't brush your teeth at the same time. If you are waiting for someone on the phone, don't attempt to look through the mail or a magazine. When someone is talking to you, put down your newspaper, magazine or work and give the person your full attention.
- Reduce your tendency to think and talk rapidly by making a conscious effort to listen to others. Become "a ready listener" (Jas. 1:19, *AMP*). Ask questions to encourage others to continue talking. If you have something to say, ask yourself, *Who really wants to hear this? Is this the best time to share it?*
- Reevaluate your need for recognition. Instead of looking for the approval of others, tell yourself in a realistic way, "I did a good job and I can feel all right about it."
- If you have the tendency to ask "How much?" and "How many?" and to think in numbers, change the way you evaluate others or situations. Express your feelings in adjectives and not numbers.
- Begin to read magazines and books that have nothing to do with your vocation. Become adventuresome, but don't see how many different books you can read—or brag to others about this "accomplishment."
- Play some soft background music at home or at the office to give a soothing atmosphere.
- Attempt to plan your schedule so that you drive or commute when traffic is light. Drive in the slow lane of the highway or freeway. Try to reduce your tendency to drive faster than others or just as fast.
- Pick days to leave your watch at home. Keep track of how often you find yourself looking at your wrist that day.
- Tape-record one of your own phone or dinner conversations and play it back. Note whether you talk most, ask questions or

listen to answers. Do you speed up your conversation by sup-plying the endings of sentences for your partner? Do you inter-rupt or change the topic to fit your needs?

- Don't evaluate your life in terms of how much you have accom-plished or how many material things you have acquired. Recall your past enjoyable experiences for a few minutes each day. Take time to daydream about pleasurable experiences as a child.

- Make your noon hour a rest time away from work. Go shop-ping, browse through stores, read or have lunch with a friend.

- Begin your day 15 minutes early and do something you enjoy. If you tend to skip breakfast or eat standing up, sit down and take your time eating. Look around the house or outside and fix your interest upon something pleasant you have been over-looking, such as flowers in bloom or a beautiful painting.

- When you arrive home, announce to others (even if it's just the cat) that the first 10 minutes belong to you. Or read while you have a cup of tea in a restaurant for 10 minutes. Ask your husband to watch the children while you take a 15-minute bath or shower before you start dinner. Make this a regular part of your day.

- This one will sound crazy, but get in the longest supermarket line to practice waiting without getting upset. Give yourself permission to be in a long line. Discover how you can make time pass pleasantly. Speculate upon the lives of those around you. Talk to them about positive things, not about how long the line is. Review pleasant memories.

- As you play games or engage in sports, whether it be racquetball, skiing or cards, do it for enjoyment and not for competition. Begin to look for the enjoyment of a good run, an outstanding rally and the good feelings that come with recreation that you have been overlooking.

- Allow yourself more time than you need for your work. Schedule ahead of time and for longer intervals. If you usually take a half hour for a task, allow 45 minutes. You will see an increase in the quality of your work.

Evaluate what you do and why you do it. Lloyd Ogilvie offers some insights on our motivations and the pressures we create:

We say, "Look, God, how busy I am!" We equate exhaustion with an effective, full life. . . . We tack up performance statistics in the hope that we are counting for something in our generation. But for what or for whom? . . . A Christian is free to stop running away from life in overinvolvement.[15]

The real answer to stress is found in applying God's Word to your life. What I have done with many counselees is to suggest they read the following passages aloud several times a day. You may want to do the same.

Then [Ezra] told them, Go your way, eat the fat, drink the sweet drink, and send portions to him for whom nothing is prepared; for this day is holy to our Lord. And be not grieved and depressed, for the joy of the Lord is your strength and stronghold (Neh. 8:10, *AMP*).

And he shall be the stability of your times, a wealth of salvation, wisdom, and knowledge; the fear of the Lord is his treasure (Isa. 33:6, *NASB*).

You will guard him and keep him in perfect and constant peace whose mind [both its inclination and its character] is stayed on you, because he commits himself to you, leans on you, and hopes confidently in you (Isa. 26:3, *AMP*).

Do not fret or have any anxiety about anything, but in every circumstance and in everything by prayer and petition [definite requests], with thanksgiving, continue to make your wants known to God (Phil. 4:6, *AMP*).

Now that we've looked at some of the information about anger, let's take a detour from it in the next two chapters and explore two related emotions that many women struggle with: fear and anxiety, and depression.

Take Action

1. List the three main stressors in your life at this time.
2. What steps can you take to deal with each one?
3. On a scale of 0 to 10, indicate where you are on the path to burnout.

0 ————————————— 5 ————————————— 10

I'm doing fine   Moderate burnout   Total burnout

4. Look back over the suggestions on how to deal with stress in your life and decide which three would help you most.

CHAPTER 8

HIGH ANXIETY

H. Norman Wright

Fay was a middle-aged, well-groomed, successful woman who came to me for counseling. She did not display the normal apprehension that so many people experience during an initial counseling session. She communicated very well, and she was alert and polished in her manner. From her appearance and accomplishments, you would never have guessed the extent of the fear festering inside her that she admitted to me that day. When I remarked about her outward control and composure, Fay replied, "*No one* is aware of the fear I live with. I am very capable of hiding it."

I asked her, "How have you accomplished so much while carrying such a load of fear?"

Fay's answer amazed me: "That's just it—I'm motivated by fear! Fear drives me; it keeps me going. I don't like being controlled by fear, but I wonder if I would accomplish anything if I were not motivated by it."

Driven by fear. I wonder how many people are driven, like Fay, by the fears of their lives. It seems like such a negative way to be motivated. In some ways a fear-driven lifestyle can be very effective. But there is a high cost for such a negative drive.

While Fay was motivated by fear, many women are immobilized and crippled by this strong emotion. But most women today struggle with some degree of fear and anxiety. Often it is tied to anger. Fear can easily turn into an anger response because anger is a less personally threatening emotion for many women: They feel less vulnerable being angry than being fearful.

Not that fear is all negative, however. It can serve a positive purpose, for it was "designed by God to give our bodies the sudden bursts of strength and speed we need in emergencies. But when fear becomes a permanent condition, it can paralyze the spirit, keeping us from taking the risks of generosity, love and vulnerability that characterize citizens of God's kingdom."[1]

We may be afraid at times, but none of us is to abound in fear. Paul wrote: "For God did not give us a spirit of timidity [fear], but a spirit of love and of self-discipline" (2 Tim. 1:7, *NIV*). We have freedom in Christ, yet we often choose to walk through life in a mobile cell of fear, shut away from people and experiences. Men and women alike do this. And there are consequences.

Fear disables. Fear shortens life. Fear cripples our relationships with others. Fear blocks our relationship with God. Fear makes life a chore.

The Enemy Defined

I've talked to some women who experience fear, some who are anxious, some who worry and a number who live constantly with all three handicaps. What's the difference between them—or is there a difference?

Our English word "fear" comes from the Old English *faer*, meaning "sudden calamity or danger." Fear has come to mean the emotional response to real or imagined danger. The Hebrew word for fear can also be translated "dread," a heavy, oppressive sensation of fear.

"Worry" comes from an Anglo-Saxon root meaning "to strangle" or "to choke." Worry is the uneasy, suffocating feeling we often experience in times of fear, trouble or problems. Worry is the unnecessary fretting and stewing that keeps our minds stirred up and our stomachs churning. When we worry, we look pessimistically into the future and think of the worst possible outcome to the situations of our lives.

Worry is asking the question "What if . . .?" and answering in a way that is usually negative. Worry pushes us to continue asking the question, but each time we embellish the answer with even more negative details. We imagine the worst case scenario. Unfortunately, worrying intensely that some unpleasant event might happen not only does not prevent it from happening but can actually help to bring it about.

When worry gains a foothold, it often turns into *anxiety*. In fact, one of the best ways to look at worry and anxiety is to see them on a continuum. It's easy for concern to turn to worry and then to anxiety.

Concern ————————— Worry —————————Anxiety

But what exactly is anxiety? A word we often interchange with fear, anxiety comes form the Latin *anxius*. To be anxious means to be troubled in mind about some uncertain event. A variation of anxius means "to press tightly or to strangle." Anxiety is often a suffocating experience.

Fear and anxiety are actually quite similar, but anxiety is a more elusive emotion. A true fear has an identifiable object of danger, either real (a burglar in the house) or imagined (a shadow that looks like a burglar). When we're anxious we have the same feeling of fear, but we don't know why. The danger is subconscious.

Anxiety is a vague, constant sense of tension over something bad that may happen. Perhaps it's best described by the verse in the book of Proverbs: "Anxiety in a man's heart weighs it down" (12:25, *AMP*). A dark cloud of uncertainty and even dread hovers about those who are anxious. Sometimes they feel as though they're losing all sense of control. This can throw them off balance and keep them from functioning. Some people may even experience anxiety attacks, which can totally immobilize them.

Those who surrender to anxiety will see their progress come to a halt. But if they learn to challenge it, they can use its energy to grow and become stronger.

Pastor Earl Lee illustrates the difference between the positive and negative uses of worry and anxiety:

If we surrender to anxiety, we will see our progress come to a halt.

Worry is like *racing* an automobile engine while it is in neutral. The gas and noise and smog do not get us anywhere. But legitimate concern . . . is putting the car into low gear on your way to moving ahead. You tell yourself that you are going to use the power God has given you to do something about the situation which could cause you to fret.[3]

The Edge of Panic

People who don't use their anxious energy to fuel their efforts for change may experience another condition that can develop along with worry and anxiety: a *phobia*. "Phobia" comes from the Greek word *phobos*, which means "flight," and is also the name of the ancient Greek deity who provoked panic and fear in his enemies. A phobia is a persistent fear of a person, object or idea that in reality doesn't justify fear. People with a phobia experience fear that is out of proportion to the situation. And this fear is beyond voluntary control: They can't stop it, can't reason or explain it away—not even if they know it's unrealistic and irrational. Such people live on the edge of panic. They become hypervigilant, always on the lookout for their particular fear. They develop what is called "preplanned avoidance," trying to avoid fear by avoiding any suspicious setting. Their entire life can be dominated by their phobia. Over time they can become prisoners of it.

If you've never experienced a phobia or don't know someone who has, you may feel it's simple to overcome. But it isn't. And the situation is complicated by the fact that many people who have phobias know their actions are irrational. This generates a fear of sharing their feelings with others. As a result, such people become even more isolated and start to think that they are the only ones who have ever experienced such fears.

Tranquil Mind, Happy Heart

Anyone who feels isolated by fear, worry and anxiety has only to pick up the Bible to be convinced that these are common human experiences. Many Scripture verses describe the ravages of fear, worry and anxiety. But many verses also reveal that a worry-free life is possible and that it reaps many positive rewards. Notice the contrast in the verses below.

> I heard, and my [whole inner self] trembled; my lips quivered at the sound. Rottenness enters into my bones and under me [down to my feet] I tremble (Hab. 3:16, *AMP*).

> A tranquil mind gives life to flesh (Prov. 14:30, *RSV*).

> All the days of the desponding and afflicted are made evil [by anxious thoughts and forebodings], but he who has a glad heart has a continual feast [regardless of circumstances] (Prov. 15:15, *AMP*).

> A happy heart is good medicine and a cheerful mind works healing, but a broken spirit dries up the bones (Prov. 17:22, *AMP*).

If you can relate to these descriptions of fear, worry and anxiety, the good news is that you can also attain a tranquil mind and happy heart, with God's help. But first, a greater degree of self-knowledge may be needed.

What Am I Afraid of?

It appears that the anxiety situations that are the most immobilizing for women are any that could lead to the loss of love. Women don't want to run the risk of being unloved—a fear that is tied into the fear of abandonment. This keeps women hooked into destructive and abusive

relationships or causes them to behave in ways that are counter to who
they really are. These women are afraid of being rejected.

Mary had this to say about her long-time struggles with such fears:

> When I am dating a man and I feel rejected, I come on too strong
> and demand love and acceptance in some way. And that chases
> him right out the door! And I know I caused the rejection. But I
> don't know what to do!
>
> That's not the only way I respond to my fear of rejection.
> Sometimes I feel real inhibited with a man, so I withdraw. I'm
> afraid of exposing my true self and being rejected. But my with-
> drawal also brings on rejection because he sees me as a real dud.
> I can't let him know that I care for him and crave his attention
> and acceptance. It's almost like I'm caught in a vicious cycle. But
> I don't know how to get out of it!

This can lead to another common fear, that of being vulnerable.
What if you're open with someone and they don't like you, or you become
so enmeshed that you lose your identity?

Women don't want to run the risk of being unloved—and so they stay in destructive and abusive relationships.

The fear of making the wrong choice
or the wrong decision is a constant companion for many women. In addition,
many struggle with the fear of depen-
dence but are also fearful of independence, or with the fear of failure but also
the fear of success. Many are afraid of not
being able to master the rules of working
in a man's world, but some are afraid of
being caught up and assimilated into
that world. Some are struggling with the
fear of being too proficient at what they
do; others fight the fear of not being
good enough. Women also feel anxiety
over the choice of either having or not having children. And more and
more women experience the tension of trying to meet the needs of all the

people in their lives, versus focusing on just one aspect of life and having to suffer the consequences for not doing everything.[4]

What Do I Do Now?

Whether your problem is fear, anxiety, worry or a combination of all three, there are four definite steps you can take that have helped many women.

Identify Your Fears, Anxieties or Worries

It's important to identify the problem as specifically as possible. One woman told me she was afraid of men. My questions helped her to pinpoint her fears: "Are you afraid of being rejected by men, of being taken advantage by men, of what they might think about you or say about you? What is it about men that makes you fearful?"

In each situation that makes you generally fearful, there can be a number of specific aspects to your fear. These must be identified. Once you have made this specific identification, you can plan a specific strategy.

Take a sheet of paper and write down a fear you have. Then list all of the different characteristics unique to that fear. Do the same with all your other fears. Some of your fears may have only one or two points, while others may have five or six. Once you have listed your specific fears, rank them in order of importance, beginning with whatever you fear most.

Yes, all this requires some work. But if you don't recognize or examine your anxiety, you can't use its energy in a positive way. And if you don't face it, you're simply putting a bandage over an untreated, festering abscess. Often the bandage is depression that keeps those anxious feelings under such control that you may not even be aware of the anxiety. But when you face the anxiety you can at least mobilize to do something, whereas depression immobilizes you.

Create a History of Your Fears and Anxieties

Once you have identified and ranked your fears on a sheet of paper, write down "Past experiences with this fear." Under this heading, describe two or three times when you actually experienced this fear or anxiety. Use the most recent experiences you can remember and give as many details as possible. Then compare your description with the list of characteristics you previously identified for this fear to see if they coincide.

Can you remember what you actually said to yourself at the time you experienced your fear? Your statements may have included, "I feel awful," "I wish I was out of here," "This is a terrible experience," or "I can't handle this." What you say to yourself is important, because it can either diminish or reinforce your fears and anxieties. Be very specific in listing your reaction to these past situations. Were you immobilized or did you run away? Were you calm or did you experience anxiety symptoms? List all of your symptoms.

Then look over what you've written and ask yourself some questions: Are these fears healthy or unhealthy? Are they rational or irrational? What are the consequences of my fears? You will discover that the step of admitting and identifying your fear will cause it to diminish.

It's like being afraid of the ghost in the closet. The longer you sit and think about it—its color, size and temperament—the more you feed your fear and the stronger it grows. But once you make the effort to grab a flashlight and look into the closet, you discover there is no ghost. Often such a fear exists only in the mind, or that's where it grows.

Become Aware of What You Are Saying to Yourself About Whatever You're Afraid of, and Learn to Challenge It

I've worked with a number of women who have struggled with the fear of rejection. The following is a list of some of the thoughts that I've heard:

- "I must make a good, positive first impression. If I don't, they will never like me or accept me." (This fear creates such hesitancy that the initial impression becomes a disaster!)
- "I need to have the perfect opening line." (This belief will keep a person from ever opening her mouth. There *is* no perfect opening line!)
- "I must be comfortable and articulate before I engage others in conversation. Otherwise, they will notice my discomfort and reject me."

How can a person counter these impossible expectations? One way is to challenge them to see if they are really true or not. Most of the time they are negative, exaggerated beliefs. Another way is to consider them in light of the truth of Scripture. The following verses can help counter the fear of rejection by showing us our true worth, and also how much we are valued and accepted.

And the Lord said to Moses, "I . . . am pleased with you and I know you by name" (Exod. 33:17, *NIV*).

Before I formed you in the womb I knew you, before you were born I set you apart (Jer. 1:5, *NIV*).

I am the good shepherd; I know my sheep and my sheep know me . . . and I lay down my life for the sheep . . . My sheep listen to my voice; I know them . . . and they shall never perish (John 10:14-15,27-28, *NIV*).

Keep in mind that while feelings of rejection breed anger and even rage, people who fear rejection do not usually express their angry feelings directly; they are afraid to bring about more rejection. And so their fear intensifies, which causes them to need even more acceptance and reassurance, which in turn causes them to respond at even deeper levels of withdrawal or demand. And so fear and anger feed one another, forming a vicious cycle that continues on and on.

> *Fear and anger feed one another, forming a vicious cycle that continues on and on.*

Face Your Fear or Anxieties

If your fear is legitimate, you can learn to face it. You can build a strong spiritual foundation and become aware of the resources God has given you.

You have already taken the important step of admitting that you are afraid and have identified the fear. Now ask yourself, "What can I do to eliminate or decrease my fear?" Usually the solution will involve facing the fear in some way. Face it—but gradually. Don't rush into it. Take it slow. Let your confidence build. Reach out for support and encouragement from others. Let someone else know what you're doing and ask for their prayer support.

Gaining the victory over fear can take time. Remember David's advice in Psalm 27:14: "Wait for the Lord; be strong, and let your heart take courage; yes, wait for the Lord" (*NASB*).

Worry—How to Master It

Is worry your particular problem? Here are 10 things you can do to conquer the worry habit. (You'll notice that some of the steps that are useful for mastering fear can also be used against worry).

Face your worries and admit them when they occur. Don't run from them, for they will return to haunt you. Don't worry about worrying. That just reinforces and perpetuates the problem.

Itemize your worries and anxieties on a sheet of paper. Be specific and complete as you describe them. Keep track of when each one occurs during the day.

Write down the reasons or causes for your worry. Investigate the sources. Is there any possibility that you can eliminate the source or cause of your worry? Have you tried? What have you tried specifically?

Write down the amount of time you spend each day worrying.

Make another list. Note (a) the way your worrying has prevented a feared situation from occurring; (b) the way your worrying has increased the problem.

Try to eliminate any sources of irritation if you are nervous or jumpy. Stay away from them until you learn how to react differently. For example, if troubling world events worry you, don't watch so many newscasts. Use that time to relax by reading, working in the garden or riding a bike for several miles. Avoid rushing yourself. If you worry about being late, plan to arrive at a destination early. Give yourself more time.

Avoid any type of fatigue—physical, emotional or intellectual. When you are fatigued, worrisome difficulties can loom out of proportion.

When you start to worry, ask yourself: "Is this something for me to worry over?" In other words, is this something that really pertains to you and your life, or does it properly belong to someone else? Remember that your fears or worries often may be disguised fears of what others think of you.

When a problem arises, face it and decide what you can do about it. Make a list of all the possible solutions and decide which you think is the best one. If these are minor decisions, make them fairly quickly. Take more time for major decisions.

A worrier usually says, "I go over and over these problems and can't decide which approach is best." Look at the facts, then make yourself decide. After you have made your decision, don't question or worry about your choice. Otherwise the worrying pattern erupts all over again. Practice this new pattern of making decisions.

Centering on God

Freedom from worry is possible! You may have practiced worrying for many years. Now you need to consistently practice applying Scripture over a long period in order to completely establish a new, worry-free pattern. If you fail, don't give up.

How do you apply Scripture? Take a 3x5-inch card and on one side write the word "Stop." On the other side, write out Philippians 4:6-9 word for word. (We use either the *Living Bible* or the *Amplified Bible*.) Keep the card with you at all times. Whenever you are alone and begin to worry, take the card out, hold the *Stop* side in front of you, and say, "Stop!" aloud twice, with emphasis. Then turn the card over and read the Scripture passage aloud twice, with emphasis.

Taking the card out interrupts your thought pattern of worry. Saying "Stop!" further breaks your automatic habit pattern of worry. Then reading the Word of God aloud becomes the positive substitute for worry. This method works, not only if you're alone, but also if you're in a group. If you're with others when you begin to worry, follow the

same procedure, only do it silently. You may also want to use Psalm
37:1-10, which begins by telling us not to fret. Be sure to study this passage. Concentrate on the positive substitutes for "fret"; "delight," "commit," "rest."

Also study Matthew 6:25-34 to discover several principles that help
to overcome anxiety and worry. First, note that Jesus did *not* say, "Stop
worrying when everything is going all right for you." He simply and
directly said to stop worrying about your life. In a way, Jesus was saying that we should learn to accept situations that can't be altered at
the present time. That doesn't mean we're to sit back and make no
attempt to improve conditions around us. But we must face tough situations without worry and learn to live with them while we work
toward improvement.

Second, Jesus said that we can't add any length of time to our life
span by worrying. Not only is this the case, but the physical effects of
worry can actually shorten our life span.

Third, the object of our worry may be part of the difficulty. Perhaps
our sense of values is distorted. Perhaps what we're worrying about
shouldn't be the center of our attention.

Fourth, Christ also recommends that we practice living a day at a
time. We may be able to change some of the results of past behavior, but
we can't change the past. Neither can we predict or completely prepare
for the future. So don't apologize over past mistakes or inhibit the
potential of the future by worrying about it. Focus your energies on the
opportunities today.

Center your thoughts on God, not on worry. Remember the words
of Isaiah, who receive in the Lord and His faithfulness: "You will guard
him and keep him in perfect and constant peace whose mind [both in
inclination and its character] is stayed on you" (Isa. 26:3, *AMP*).
Whatever you choose to think about will either produce or dismiss
feelings of anxiety and worry. Center your mind on the negative
thoughts and always anticipate the worst, and you will suffer from
worry. Center your mind or imagination on God—what He has done
and will do for you—and on the promises of Scripture, and peace of
mind is inevitable.

The choice is yours. You must choose whether or not you will center your thoughts this way. God has made the provision, but you must take the action. Freedom from worry and anxiety is available, but you must lay hold of it![5]

Take Action

Here are some common fears that keep us from honestly saying what we want or doing what we know is best. Read through this list slowly and thoughtfully. Consider the degree and impact of each type of fear on your current choices and relationships. Check any of these fears that hold you back.

_____ Fear of hurting someone
_____ Fear of rejection, criticism or disapproval
_____ Fear of physical abuse, attack or intimidation
_____ Fear of conflict or making matters worse
_____ Fear of failure or making a mistake
_____ Fear of taking risks or facing insecurity
_____ Fear of making a scene or losing control
_____ Fear of what other people think or say
_____ Fear of embarrassment or humiliation
_____ Fear of abandonment or aloneness
_____ Fear of inadequacy or not being up to what the situation demands
_____ Fear of intimacy or vulnerability

If your fear isn't listed, write it down.

For each fear that you have listed, respond to the following questions and statements:

1. When was the first time you became aware of this fear?
2. The reason it developed was . . .
3. This fear occurs most often when . . .
4. The response I want to replace this fear with is . . .
5. The step I will take is . . .

CHAPTER 9

DEPRESSION: THE FLIP SIDE OF ANGER

H. Norman Wright

You probably already know what it's like to be depressed. But depression is not like the sadness from a disappointment or loss. In a short while this feeling lifts, and even when it's your companion you still function well. Depression is different: It lasts longer and is more intense. It lingers with its immobilizing intensity, causing you to lose perspective and making you less able to carry on your activities. The loss of perspective that accompanies depression colors the way you experience your life, your tasks and your family.

When you're depressed you experience changes in physical activities—eating, sleeping, sex. Some lose interest in food, while others attempt to set a world record at gorging themselves. Some sleep constantly; others cannot sleep. If a lessening of sexual interest occurs, depression may be the cause. Whatever the particular effects, depression interferes with your ability to function. And your impaired functioning only creates more depression.

Your self-esteem and self-confidence are low. You withdraw from others because of a fear of being rejected. Unfortunately, when you're depressed your behavior does bring on some rejection from others. You cancel favorite activities, fail to return phone calls and seek ways to avoid talking with or seeing others. Not only do you want to avoid people: you also desire to escape from problems, and even from life itself. Thoughts of leaving home or running away, suicidal thoughts and wishes—all these arise because of your feeling that life is hopeless and worthless.

When depressed, you're oversensitive to what others say and do. You may misinterpret actions and comments in a negative way. These mistaken perceptions can make you irritable and cause you to cry easily.

You have difficulty handling most of your feelings, especially anger. Often this anger is directed outward, against others. But it can also be misdirected toward yourself: You feel worthless and don't know how to deal with the situation. Guilt is usually present at a time of depression. The basis for it may be real or imagined. Frequently guilt feelings arise because you assume that you're in the wrong somehow or that your depression is responsible for making others miserable. Depression distorts our perception of life.

Richard F. Berg, a therapist, describes our ability to perceive as similar to a camera. Photographers can alter the image of reality through the use of various lenses or filters. For example, a wide-angle lens gives a broad panorama but the objects appear more distant and smaller than they really are. A telephoto lens can focus on a beautiful flower, but in so doing it shuts out the rest of the garden. Happy and smiling people seen through a fish-eye lens appear distorted and unreal. Filters can blur reality, break up images into pieces, bring darkness into a lighted scene or even create a mist. Like photographers' lenses and filters, depression distorts our perception of the world. Depression is like a set of camera filters that focus on the darker portions of life and take away the warmth, action and joy from a scene. A photographer is aware of the distortion created by switching lenses. The depressed person, however, is not very aware of the distortion that he or she is creating as the lenses are switched. When we are depressed we are partially blind without knowing it. And the more intense our depression, the greater the distortion.[1]

Depression: What You Need to Know

In simple terms, depression is merely a negative emotion. However, it may also be a sign of serious, even malignant, disease. Depression is a term that can describe the "blahs" or the "blues"—or it can describe a neurotic or psychotic disorder. Depression can be mild, moderate or severe. It can be harmless or life-threatening. Depression can be an inspiration to some creative people, or it can end in suicide for others. Depression can be a disorder, or merely a symptom of a disorder.

Depression can be found in babies less than 1 year old and in people who are over 100 years old. In some individuals, depression may be readily observed by any layperson; in others it may be so masked that only experts can recognize it.

Depression can be caused by physical, mental, emotional or spiritual problems, or by a combination of these. It can be caused by our self-defeating thinking or by separation from God. But it can also result from a shortage of malfunctioning of essential neurotransmitters in the brain. Standard causes of depression include fatigue, insufficient or improper food, insufficient rest, reaction to medications, glandular imbalance, PMS, hypoglycemia, food allergies, low self-esteem, a pattern of negative thinking, behavior that contradicts your values and postpartum issues. Depression can result from major variables in atmospheric pressure, or perhaps lack of sunlight during the late fall and winter.

Depression Has a Silver Lining

Is it abnormal to be depressed? Not at all. There has always been depression and there always will be. You're not alone in it. In fact, you're in good company. Many of the people God used mightily in the Old Testament were so depressed they wanted to die—Moses, for example, and Job, Elijah, Jonah and writers of the Psalms (see especially Pss. 42 and 43). Great men and women throughout history have struggled with depres-

sion, so don't believe that it's a sin to be depressed, or that Christians
don't experience depression. That is just not true! Depression is a normal
response to what is occurring in our life. I've always liked the way
Archibald Hart describes the positive side of depression.

> Depression is like pain. While pain is inconvenient, it is a warning system, essential for our survival. . . . If I felt no pain, I'd be killed the first day I walked out my front door. God also has created me with the ability to experience depression so that I can have a very important warning system to tell me when things are wrong.[2]

A depression is healthy when you have actual feelings of pain, sadness and disappointment from the negative experiences of life.

A new way of describing depression, which makes it easier to understand, is to distinguish between healthy and unhealthy depression. A depression is healthy when you have *actual* feelings of pain, sadness and disappointment (which may also include guilt, anger and anxiety) from the negative experiences of life. This could include traumas, losses, discrimination, unfair treatment, and any past hurt or damage that is still unresolved. When depressed in this way you can still function, but not as well as you normally do.

Unhealthy depression, on the other hand, is an *inability to function* in any of the more basic areas of life—work, relationships, body functions and so on—because of the depth of your bad feelings. It can arise from a multitude of factors, including too many painfully unresolved experiences, genetic vulnerability and changes in body chemistry.

One main distinction between healthy and unhealthy depression is the fact that healthy depressions are not usually biological in nature. Another main distinction is the degree to which the depressed person can function. Healthy depressions are less severe and can usually be resolved without professional help. Awareness and action are the key ingredients. You *can* face the world. But when you experience an unhealthy depression, you usually shut down as well as shut out the world.[3]

Are Women More Prone to Depression Than Men?

What about it? Are women more prone to depression than men? It appears so. At least two-thirds of those who are depressed are women, and some studies indicate that the ratio may be as high as six to one.[4] Why is this? Any loss can trigger a reactive depression. It could be an actual concrete loss involving something tangible: a person, a job, a home, a car, a valued photograph, a pet. The stronger the attachments, the more intense the feelings of loss. Especially devastating for women—because they put so much of themselves into relationships and build strong attachments—are the losses of any love relationship. Also potentially devastating are those losses that take place only in your mind—the loss of love, hope, ambition, self-respect or other intangible elements of life. It could even be a dream that disappears.

Unrealistic expectations can also make us prone to depression; the higher our ideal is above the real, the greater our letdown will be.

The most difficult type of loss to handle, however, is the threatened loss. This loss has not yet occurred, but there is a real possibility that it will happen. Waiting for the results of a biopsy or a state bar exam, waiting to hear from the admissions office of a college to which you have applied—situations like this carry the possibility of loss. Depression can arise because we feel powerless to do anything about the situation. In a sense we are immobilized by threatened losses, overshadowed by depression. It is difficult to accept or deal with a loss that hasn't yet occurred.

I've talked with many women who experience depression during the crucial transitions of life that take place during the 20s, 30s and 40s. It is difficult for a woman to know if she has made the right decisions. And then in the middle years there are other losses. A woman can lose her mother role, identity source and physical attractiveness. She may grieve over not having become the person she might have been.[5]

Both anger and guilt, mentioned earlier as companions of depression, can also cause depression. Unrecognized or unexpressed anger turns its fury inward looking for an object to punish; in this case it's yourself. Men tend to be more aggressive with their feelings, but if assertion is difficult for you, then you will tend to withdraw, feel powerless, see the internally and become depressed.

Unrealistic expectations can also make us prone to depression; the higher our ideal is above the real, the greater our letdown will be. Unrealism can be an issue in beliefs about ourselves, others or even our faith. Often it is a factor in relationships with men. And unmet expectations can lead to anger, which if left undealt with, leads to depression.

Can Depression Be Inherited?

Inherited depression has been defined as sad or bad feelings that occur when biological, genetic, cultural or psychological depressions exist in a family and are passed down to the next generation as an increased vulnerability to both healthy and unhealthy depression. Sometimes this is disguised so well it's hard to discern. The factors that are the most difficult to identify as depression are biological or genetic, or both. The symptoms may come out as addictions, eating disorders or psychosomatic disorders. The tendency to depression can also be passed down by example, since people learn by example and observation. Relatives can pass down depressive ways of thinking and even behaving.[6]

Who in *your* family tree was depressed? Who were the people, especially your women relatives, who were depressed? You might find it very helpful to think about and research this. While you're at it, ask yourself where *you* would fall on this scale currently . . . five years ago . . . as an adolescent ... as a child. How much change, loss, stress, disappointment, physical illness or trauma have you experienced in the past two years? In the last year? How have you responded to each situation? What type of support did you experience from others? Was there any anger associated with any of the events; if so, what did you do with it? Was it converted into depression?

How likely is it that depression will have an impact on your life? As a woman you have at least a one in four chance of experiencing a major unhealthy depression.[7] If your relatives, especially women, experienced severe neurotic depression or manic depression, you are two to three times more likely than others to experience these depressions as well.

If there are depression symptoms such as alcoholism or drug abuse among close relatives, you're eight to ten times more likely to develop similar symptoms.[8] If a close relative committed suicide, you will be more vulnerable to suicide, should you experience depression.[9]

What does all this mean? *Don't ignore your depression. Don't ignore your anger.* Be aware. Look for alternatives to the way you are responding.

What to Do with Your Depression

Keep in mind that this complex and confusing malady called depression has a purpose: to alert you to whatever is causing the problem so you can eliminate the cause.

The initial step is to admit that what you are experiencing is depression. Put a name to it and don't ignore what is taking place in your life.

Then check for any physical reasons for your depression. You may want to see your medical doctor for this.

If there is no physical cause, then your next step is to ask yourself two key questions. You may even want to ask your mate or a good friend to help you think them through:

1. Am I doing anything that might be contributing to my depression? Check your behavior to determine that it is consistent with Scripture and your values.

2. About what, or in what way, am I thinking that could be contributing to my depression? Is there a correlation with anger?

Look for your depression "trigger." Some triggers are obvious and you're
readily aware of what prompted the depression. Other causes are more
difficult to discover. To help you track them down, you may want to
write the following questions on a card: What did I do? Where did I go?
With whom did I speak? What did I see? What did I read? What was I
thinking? Refer to this card when you're depressed; it may help you
recall the thought or event that triggered the depression.

Please do not attempt to deal with your depression by yourself. If the
depression has been with you for some time, talk to a trusted friend and
seek out a professional Christian counselor. But do something.

How Can You Get a New Perspective?

Can you imagine your life being better after your depression than
before? Unlikely though it may seem, many have experienced just that.
Remember the passage in the last chapter of Job? "And the Lord blessed
the latter days of Job more than his beginning" (Job 42:12, NASB).
Through your depression, you can develop a new perspective about life,
a greater awareness of your identity and your abilities, a new way of seeing and relating to others, and a deeper relationship with God.

This latter step occurs as you feed on His Word, especially on verses
like these:

Keep me safe, O God, for in you I take refuge (Ps. 16:1, NIV).

The Lord is my light and my salvation—whom shall I fear? The
Lord is the stronghold of my life—of whom shall I be afraid? (Ps.
27:1, NIV).

Reflecting on God's Word will reveal the truth about who you are
and who God is—and this is the basis for changing your perception of
who you are. God is committed to performing good in our lives.

Take Action

1. Identify a time when you were depressed as an adolescent, a young adult and in the past three years. What were the causes?
2. List the major losses you have experienced in your life. Which of them is still affecting your life?
3. When you are depressed, what do you do to cope?
4. When you are depressed, what do you do to resolve it?
5. Identify what you have learned about yourself from your depression.
6. What constructive steps will you take the next time you are depressed?

CHAPTER 10

HARASSED AND ABUSED— YOU NEED TO BE ANGRY!

H. Norman Wright

Susan Forward and Joan Torres, in *Men Who Hate Women and the Women Who Love Them*, define abuse this way: "*Abuse* is any behavior that is designed to control and/or subjugate another person through the use of fear, humiliation and verbal or physical assaults. In a sense, it is the systematic persecution of one family member by another."[1] Fists and feet are the weapons of physical abuse, whereas words and looks are the weapons of emotional abuse.

Physical abuse is some form of brutal physical contact that is purposeful rather than accidental. It can include any behavior that either intends to inflict or actually does inflict physical harm. The varieties include pushing, grabbing, shoving, slapping, kicking, biting, choking, punching, hitting with an object or attacking with a knife or a gun. I will never forget the first abuse victim I saw. Her husband had beaten her head against the bathroom floor and pulled out patches of her hair.

Emotional abuse has a multitude of expressions. Scare tactics, insults, yelling, temper tantrums, name-calling and continuous criticism fall into this classification. Threatened violence is a form of emotional abuse, too. Holding up a weapon, swinging a fist near your face, destroying property or kicking your cat falls into this category. Withholding privileges or affection or constantly blaming you for the family's difficulties is abuse.

Who Abuses—And Why?

Is there a person in your life who abuses you? It could be a father, husband or boyfriend. Or it might be another woman. Although the material in this chapter deals mainly with abusive men, keep in mind that women can be abusive as well. It can occur with their husband, children or even parents.

Men who come from homes in which they experienced a violent and abusive childhood are more likely to abuse their spouse or girlfriend. Abusers typically were abused personally, or they witnessed the abuse of a parent. When verbal or physical abuse is the pattern for settling disputes and conflict within a family, the children are limited in their opportunity to learn alternative ways of expressing their anger. They continue the pattern because it's what they know best.

Men who abuse often have difficulty not only in expressing their feelings but also in identifying and dealing with them when they occur. All too often, whether the feeling is fear, frustration or anxiety, the only way they can let it out is through anger. Often they have difficulty showing affection, and it too ends up being expressed through abuse.

A man may use his inexpressiveness as a power tool to dominate others. When he's silent, who knows what he's thinking? Who is willing to shatter the calm by rocking the boat? So family members go along with what he wants rather than risk unleashing what may be inside him. When inexpressiveness isn't working, he can use actual physical abuse to vent his inner rage and control others that way.

Many studies indicate that abusive men are usually nonassertive away from home and struggle with low self-esteem. Their behavior within the home reflects this. In feeling poorly about themselves and not living up to our society's portrayal of what a man should be, they exceed what is normal behavior and become abusive.[2]

Abusive men have rigid beliefs about the roles of husbands and wives. Often a wife becomes socially isolated and then has to become dependent on her abusive husband for emotional support. He believes that a husband should be the absolute, autocratic leader in the home. Unfortunately, I have encountered Christian men who misinterpret and misuse Scripture to substantiate this belief. This view of a man's role also includes the view that he should never appear to be weak; should never ask others for help; should be the one to make all family decisions; should be "honored and respected" in all ways by his family; and should always be in control of his emotions. He expects his wife to be both submissive and inferior in all areas.[3] In other words, he has a distorted view of what a man is and what Scripture teaches.

One last characteristic is not surprising. Many abusers have difficulty with substance and alcohol abuse, especially the latter.

Who Tolerates Abuse—And Why?

What are the women like who tolerate abuse? Is there a pattern? Those who are abused have many characteristics in common, but of course there are exceptions to what is stated here. Many women will not tolerate this behavior and either intervene in a successful way or immediately terminate the relationship.

Like the abuser, an abused woman often comes from an abusive family background and has a poor self-image. Many accept abuse as normal behavior because they were raised in an abusive home, and they may blame themselves for the abuse they experience.

A woman who is abused tends to have low self-esteem, and this feeling makes her easy prey to her husband's abuse. The emotional abuse of threats, ridicule, put-downs and criticism is devastating and feeds her feelings of low self-esteem. If you hear a negative, repetitive tirade over a period of time, you begin to believe the statements. Many women end up believing that they don't deserve anything better. They become "pleasers," attempting to meet the needs of everyone in the family except themselves.

> *Like the abuser, an abused woman often comes from an abusive family background and has a poor self-image.*

If you are being abused, you're probably holding on to an unrealistic hope. You believe that in time, if you're patient and faithful, your abusing man will change. You accept every promise he gives, and since the times when abuse is absent are good, you do have a taste of what you have always hoped for.

One of my clients, Judy, had been coming to counseling for several weeks. One day she arrived and said, "I'm not sure that I need to come for counseling anymore. Jim has done such a dramatic turnaround and seems to be living up to his promise of not abusing me anymore. I think he really means it this time. And when he isn't abusive the relationship is so wonderful."

My reply was a twofold question. "Judy, how long has it been since he was abusive toward you, and how many other times has he said he wouldn't do it again?" I already knew the answer from our previous discussions. As soon as I asked, the smile left her face as she too remembered the litany of broken promises. It had been only 10 days since the last abuse had occurred.

If you're abused, you tend to isolate yourself over the months and years. You begin to isolate yourself socially because you are afraid that others will discover your situation and because your husband prefers that you be available at all times. In time, you will become so cut off that you'll be unaware that you have any other alternative. Then you become more enmeshed in the abusive pattern.

Dependency, both emotional and economic, tends to keep you locked into this relationship. If you have little education or few work skills, you're probably afraid of being left without anything. If you work, who controls your money? The chances are, your husband.

One of the tragedies in this situation is the loss of healthy boundaries. Abused women lose the *sense* of objectivity needed to make the determination that they're in any danger. The abuse becomes so common that even blood, bruises and pain don't signal that their personal boundaries have been invaded.

One of the most difficult problems for abused women may be that they cling to a traditional role in marriage. This is not wrong in itself, unless a woman tries to save her marriage even though her husband is a threat to her and the children, believing wives should tolerate transgressions in order to be loving and submissive.

If your marriage isn't working, you may believe it's your task to fix it, and if your self-worth is tied up in the success of your marriage, it's easy to why you're under so much bondage to make it work. To you, divorce would be a sign of failure. That belief, coupled with cultural Christian values and perhaps your coming from a divorced home, keeps you where you are.[4] Sometimes, though, a temporary separation of residence is needed to convince your partner that he is harming both the marriage and his family.

What Can You Do If You Are Being Abused

What can you do now? What if you find yourself in this situation or you know someone who is?

If your spouse is currently physically abusing you (or any family member), take the steps necessary to remove yourself from the setting where you are being victimized. This assumes that you have tried on your own through proper confrontation or even using a family and friend's intervention program, and nothing has changed. Remember that you are a valuable, chosen person, and your body is a temple of the Holy Spirit. Don't let others mistreat you; no one deserves abuse. If you are in a church that tells you to stay in an abusive environment, find another church.

Go immediately for professional help. The person or agency can assist you with the following steps. (1) Find out what the laws are about abuse and what legal steps you can take. You need to know your legal status and options, spouse abuse or child abuse laws, police procedures, and victim options. (2) Devise a safety plan for you and any other abused person(s). This should include a safe environment—one that is accepting, nonthreatening and protective. Develop a plan to get to the safe environment, including the best timing, transportation, money, clothes and so on. (3) Develop a network of other people to rely on and who can support you.[5]

After removing yourself from the threat, focus on changing your life so that you do not become a victim again. This will take courage, but change in our lives happens when we allow the Holy Spirit to give us strength and courage. Get in touch with all of the feelings you have about being abused. Write them out. If you don't feel any anger, something is amiss. Focus on what has been done to you and how wrong it is and the injustice of it all.

If you are the victim of verbal or emotional abuse, decide and define what you want from the abuser instead of abuse. You might decide that you want to be listened to, spoken to with courtesy and kindness, respected, understood and that you want to have your opinions acknowledged.

Then decide what you want to stop permitting in your relationship. It is important that you become quite specific at this point. You might say:

- "I won't permit him to swear at me."
- "I won't permit him to insult me."
- "I won't permit him to yell at me."
- "I won't permit him to berate me in public."
- "I won't permit him to tear down my self-esteem."
- "I won't permit him to try to control me."

Then you must decide what statements you will make to your abuser. As you think of those statements, you may also begin to experience fear and panic just over the thought of saying them. You can get over the panic and fear, however. Use new assertive statements that conclude by pointing out acceptable behavior, such as, "It's not acceptable for you to speak to me in this way. The way you can talk to me is . . ."

Pick out one of the statements and sit facing an empty chair. Practice saying it out loud to the empty chair and imagine your abuser reacting to your statement. This will create a number of emotional responses on your part, but the more you practice, the more confident you will become and the more your emotional stress will lessen. Remember that when you do respond with your assertive responses, you don't have to provide any reasons for why you are saying this. As your abuser asks different questions, use the broken record technique and simply repeat what you said the first time. Stay away from debates and arguments. We have found that it is also helpful to practice or rehearse your response with a trusted friend.

In place of thinking (as so many do), What is wrong with me that he treats me like this? *think,* What's wrong with him that he's treating me this way? And whenever you see the behavior you want, reinforce it with thank-yous and praise. Such phrases might include "I really appreciate that," or "Thank you for your consideration" or "That really draws me to you when you talk to me like this!"[6]

Understanding Sexual Harassment

The term "sexual harassment" is explosive today. You hear about it weekly if not daily in some form of the media. Even if you have never yet experienced it, it's happened to someone you know. Maybe it happened to you and you weren't even aware it occurred. It can happen anywhere. Now that I understand it better, I remember incidents in high school when sexual harassment occurred between male teachers and girls in our class. It's rampant in the work area.

In October 1991 the results of a poll by the National Association of Female Executives were released. Seventy-seven percent of all those polled stated that sexual harassment was a problem in the workplace, and 55 percent said it had happened to them. However 64 percent did not report it. Of those who did, most felt that the issue was not addressed satisfactorily. They were fired or forced either to resign or to transfer to a position they did not want.[7] Most cases of sexual harassment are not reported because the woman feels so degraded, is too uncertain of her rights and options or lives in fear of retaliation.

What exactly is sexual harassment? It refers to a wide range of behavior—all of it illegal. Sexual harassment is deliberate or continual behavior or a sexual or sex-based nature that is unwelcome, not asked for and not returned. It is deliberate and repeated and can be verbal, nonverbal or physical. It can include sexual comments, jokes, suggestions or innuendos. Nonverbal harassment is quite common and includes suggestive looks, leering or ogling, blocking a woman's path or making a woman fear she's going to be grabbed.

Actual physical harassment can include "accidental" as well as deliberate action. "Accidentally" brushing up against a woman as well as "friendly" pats, squeezes or pinches are considered minor deliberate steps. But the harassment can become very serious. It can range from direct fondling and rubbing to a woman being forced to sleep with her boss or employer in order to keep her job.

Why is it so difficult for some women to speak up? There are numerous reasons. Guilt, shame, embarrassment or the fear of being labeled by others as an overreactor or an agitator or as being too sensitive or hysterical could all be factors. The woman's upbringing may make the very subject too painful or upsetting for her to face. Some women may even think that sexual harassment is just part of life and women have to learn to handle it. Some women have said they don't think it will do any good to report someone, or they're unclear about or don't trust the procedures to follow in doing so.

But perhaps there are deeper or more significant reasons tied into tradition and culture. Women have long been considered the ones responsible for controlling the level of sexual involvement. They are looked to for setting the boundaries, so when harassment happens often a woman wonders, *What have I done wrong?*

Stopping Sexual Harassment

If sexual harassment is occurring in your life, your goal is to get it stopped immediately. If it's happening at work, your goal is to get it stopped *and* keep your job as well as your potential for advancement.

Here are some issues to consider and some steps you can take.

- No matter what the behavior is or how infrequently it occurs, it's a problem that won't go away.
- Be sure you admit that a problem exists; don't deny it to yourself. You may choose, as a tactic, to ignore it and see if it goes away. Choosing to ignore it is quite different from denying that it's happening to you.
- Recognize sexual harassment for what it is—deliberate or repeated sexual behavior and control that's unwelcomed by you. Is it repeated over and over? Does your harasser know it's unwelcome? Have you said or indicated that you don't like it? Exactly what have you said? Do you participate in or initiate the behavior, such as telling off-color jokes yourself or smiling when you're saying no to his advances?
- No matter what kind of harassment it is, it's very costly to everybody. You pay a cost with a higher stress level, and your job efficiency and effectiveness are most likely affected too. It needs to be stopped immediately.

> *Deal with the harassment as soon as it occurs. Calmly, and in private, speak up and tell the person you don't like his behavior.*

- Remember that your company has an interest in stopping harassment at work. Sexual harassment damages a company or business in terms of absenteeism, loss of productivity, and lowered morale and motivation.
- Deal with the harassment as soon as it occurs. Calmly, and in private, speak up and tell the person you don't like his behavior. Aim for a relaxed, confident stance. Do not hunch or strut. Take time to adjust your position so that you're looking neither up nor down at him. The tone of your voice should be even and firm. Look him in the eye. If standing, stand at a distance

that feels comfortable—not too close, not so far that you have to raise your voice unnaturally. Make only appropriate gestures. Do not wring your hands, look down, stare, move in toward the person, or shake your finger under his nose. This poise and restraint in your gestures usually works best, especially if it's the first time you've said something about the offense and if it's a less serious behavior.

• Use an "I" statement, saying, for example: "When you call me 'one' (touch me, tell me jokes—describing the behavior you don't like), I feel very upset (embarrassed, angry, offended—saying what your feelings are) because I want to be taken seriously (want to be treated as an equal, want respect—saying why it bothers you)." Don't smile, touch the person or give any mixed messages. Don't use humor. Sometimes it helps to write out your "I" statements and rehearse them ahead of time.

• Use the broken-record technique by acknowledging the person's response and then repeating your statement. If the offender responds by saying that he didn't mean to hurt your feelings or that you're too sensitive, you can say, "I understand that you didn't mean to hurt my feelings; however, when you [state the offense] I felt [state your feelings] because [state your rationale]." You do not need to change your original "I" statement.

• Request what you do or don't want by saying "Please always call me by name (don't touch me, don't tell me those jokes)." Be specific. If the harasser persists in the unwanted behavior, make an escalated assertion, something like: "I've told you three times that I am not interested in any other relationship. I want you to stop asking me." Try this miniplan once or twice. If you don't get results from the offending employee, you'll have to do more.

• Ask a coworker for support and even help in talking with the offender. Sometimes the offender can hear a message more clearly from another person or when there is more than one person present.

- If the harassment persists, write the person a letter, spelling out what behavior you object to and why. Be sure to specify what you want to happen next. If you feel the situation is serious or bound to escalate, let him know that you will take action against the harassment if it doesn't stop at once. If your company has a written policy against harassment, you may want to attach a copy of it to your letter.[8]
- Keep a journal documenting events that occur at work, school or home.
- This can include person-to-person situations or telephone incidents. Indicate what is done and said to you and the frequency.
- Go to a supervisor, manager or owner to get additional help if the behavior does not stop. If the problem is the employer, get legal advice to see what your options are.
- Don't assume the harassment will stop if you ignore it. Seventy-five percent of the time, sexual harassment problems intensify and get worse when ignored. The person is getting away with it, so why should he stop?
- Don't try to deal with severe harassment alone, even the first time. Let your friends and family know. In serious cases, let someone in the company know about it immediately.
- If a simple plan doesn't work, or if the problem is more complex or serious, a more thorough plan might be called for. In that case, it's important to find and maintain your balance and perspective by looking at all the elements of the problem.
- Make your plans specific with regard to time, place and actions. Think through all the consequences of each plan. Keep in mind that you have two simultaneous goals at this point: to get the behavior stopped and to maintain your effectiveness in your job.
- A group approach can be effective if this problem is happening to several women. You may think you are the only one and be embarrassed to tell others. They may be thinking the very same thing! Don't handle it all alone, especially with harassers who seem to be insensitive or malicious. Call on those friends, supervisors or managers who might be able to help.

• Keep your plans flexible. The response of the harasser or the manager or company representative may change your plans or timetable.[9]

Be careful of falling into the trap of thinking that all men are abusers or harassers. They're not. And those who are abusers need to hear the message that it will no longer be tolerated. Perhaps that will shock them and encourage them to deal with their own problem areas and the confused set of values that feeds this behavior.

Remember that God created you with value, worth and dignity. If a man invades your boundaries, you have every right to stop him. In doing so you will be stopping abuse and harassment not only for yourself but for other women as well.

Take Action

1. Who are the people that you know who have been abused or sexually harassed?
2. What could you do to assist them?
3. Are there any ways in which you have been abused or harassed?
4. Are there any steps you need to take about this in your life now?

CHAPTER 11

ANGER IN THE FAMILY YOU CAME FROM

H. Norman Wright

You were born with the capacity to be angry, but somewhere you learned what to do with it. That somewhere was your family. Your family passed on to you a legacy of anger expression. It may have been healthy—and then again, it may not have been.

A number of women have told me they were thankful their parents showed their anger openly. They said, "It helped me accept my anger, and they demonstrated an appropriate display of what to do with that irritation." Other women have told me, "Mom didn't ever tell me not to be angry but instead guided me to express it in healthy ways. That I appreciate." But many others don't appreciate what they saw and heard about anger. They either saw anger out of control or lived in a repressed, avoidant type of atmosphere. Whatever pattern was there, it influenced you.

In our national survey we asked this question: As a child, the primary ways that you saw anger expressed were. . . . Here is a sampling of the responses:

- "Mean" talking (rejection)
- Loud voices, door slamming
- Quiet "steaming up"
- Raised voices, foot stomping, clapping of hands together (Mom), silence (Dad)
- Shaming and sarcastic expressions
- Yelling, tears
- I usually wasn't allowed to show anger.
- Loud voices; my father hit my mother; she became cold and distant.
- My father was semi-abusive, would call us names, spank us, shove us into walls; my mother would scream, hit cabinets, hit us with a brush on the bottom, my sibs (the two older hated each other) and I tried to mediate.
- My mother would say I never saw anger as a child because she was never angry; I think she's wrong.
- Parents wouldn't speak to each other; my sister and I would argue.
- Physical abuse, verbal abuse; in our family, feelings were not ever spoken of, everyone was always interrupting.
- Screaming; sometimes objects were thrown (my mother was volatile and explosive; my father was passive and very slow to anger).
- Voices were silenced; distance; sleep; work very hard; depression, illness (physical); tears; loud, fast talking, blaming and then release; sometimes we or my parents would talk about it and then move on.

Denial of Anger

Of all the unhealthy displays of anger in a home, the worst is when anger is purposely avoided and not expressed.

Many homes give the appearance of stability and healthy interaction. From all outward appearances the parents appear calm, consistent and balanced. But anger still exists. You find it in the parents' tight lips, piercing looks and painful and punishing silence that makes the children feel cut off from their love. The children don't express their anger. They wouldn't dare. It's forbidden. They are taught, "Not only do you not show your anger, you don't feel it either." As if that were possible!

These children are being taught a life-debilitating pattern of denial. You may have learned this pattern as a child. Or, as an adult, you may be teaching your own child this behavior. But the denial of any emotion leads to an accumulation of it. Soon there is an overabundance, with no proper avenue of drainage. Denying an emotion means you have turned its energy back against yourself and are slowly destroying yourself and your potential.

Does this sound familiar? To help you decide, let me clarify what is meant by the term "anger avoidance." It's a pattern of thinking, acting and feeling in which a person tries to ignore, avoid and suppress his or her anger.

Some families can be described as *anger-avoidant*. Either all or most of the family constantly works at minimizing their expressions of anger. Often the children carry this pattern with them and perpetuate it in their own families; if their spouses are the opposite, the pattern creates tremendous tension.

In an anger-avoidant family at least one parent models the pattern. The children are perceptive enough to see that this parent lives in fear of his or her own anger or is repulsed by any show of anger. They learn to see anger as bad, dangerous or shameful—or all of these.

Why do families follow this pattern? For many, this is their way of attempting to keep the family together and functioning. When anger is expressed it threatens the stability and functioning of the family; family members might distance themselves from each other or anger might rage out of control. One or both parents may believe that anger is always going to be destructive. In some of these families the pattern is maintained because of the false belief that the other family members don't have the ability to cope with anger. The worst possible consequences are imagined. Anger is thus infused with more power, and especially negative power, than is warranted.

Mechanisms Deployed Against Anger

In these families various mechanisms to defend against anger are employed. Family members fail to notice when others are irritated. Looks and tone of voice that carry anger are overlooked and denied. Feelings of annoyance are repressed or denied.

Conflict is bound to arise in any marriage or family relationship. But in these families conflict is not seen as normal. It threatens the stability of the family. Therefore, it must be dangerous.

If two family members were to sit and talk about their differences, that might lead to anger. So family members avoid, appease and accommodate. They avoid anything controversial and give in to others as much as possible. Thus family members learn that any expression of anger can work to get them what they want.

An anger-avoider wears blinders concerning his or her own initial feelings of irritation and annoyance. So the feelings are stuffed with the hope they'll do a disappearing act. But it doesn't work.

Manipulation becomes a byword in these families, since direct requests and confrontations are avoided. If you ask, someone might become angry. And if your request is refused, you could become angry. So the family begets members who become well versed in hinting, playing the martyr and especially in being a passive-aggressive. (This behavior pattern was described in chapter 1). Family members learn to hook one another into negative behavior patterns.

A dangerous pattern evolves in these families that tends to reinforce the myths about anger already in existence. An anger-avoider wears blinders concerning his or her own initial feelings of irritation and annoyance. To recognize them would be admitting to anger, and this is unacceptable. So the feelings are stuffed with the hope they'll do a disappearing act. But it doesn't work. When the container is filled, it spills over. When this out-of-control anger is visible it only serves to validate the person's worst fears. As one woman said, "I've always lived in fear of my anger, that if I ever did get angry I would lose control—and I did. I was right to be afraid of anger, and especially when it was over such a small thing." That is a common statement from any anger-avoider.

Once in a while a family like this actually allows one or more of its members to express their anger. Perhaps this family believes that fathers always get angry or that anger is a characteristic of a hyperactive child, a drinker, an overworked mother and so on.[1]

Often the members of these anger-avoidant families have a high number of physiological complaints as well as depression. Resentment soon develops from the buried anger and it has to have some outlet. It festers out of sight like a splinter under the skin, finally erupting in an alternative channel of expression—depression or a physical ailment.

You may feel as though you're the first person in your family to struggle with anger, but you're neither the first nor the last. If anger is a problem for you, it was a problem in previous generations as well. What you are struggling with is part of your family legacy that others also struggled with. That's why doing a family history on your family's emotions, especially anger, is so important. If you don't know about and understand your family's emotional history, you are more likely to repeat the patterns, regardless of their healthiness, or unconsciously react to them. If this is the case, you have not determined who you are or what you want for your own identity. Reflect for a moment on your family. Answer these questions either from your own memories or by tapping into memories of other family members—siblings, aunts, uncles or other significant and knowledgeable individuals.

When did your father get angry?
How did he express his anger?
Toward whom did he usually express it?
How long did it last?

What were the results at that time?
What is its effect upon you today?

When did your mother get angry?
How did she express her anger?
Toward whom did she usually express it?
How long did it last?
What were the results?
What is its effect upon you today?

When did a sibling get angry?
How did he or she express anger?
Toward whom did he or she usually express it?
How long did it last?
What were the results at that time?
What is its effect upon you today?

Glimpses of Family Life

Jean gave me a fascinating account of anger in her family that is all too common.

> You've heard of people being appointed an ambassador to a foreign country and representing their own country? Well, I received an appointment to represent my family, but it wasn't a pleasant one. I was appointed as the "angry family member." I can recall that even when I was constantly being told I was the angry one in the family—even when I wasn't! In time I just figured if that's what they wanted me to be, I'd go along with it. But over the years I discovered that I was the only one who expressed anger. At times I got the feeling they were waiting for me to get angry so they would feel better. They would provoke me until I got angry. I finally figured out they were releasing their own anger through me! I'd become the designated anger bearer! I wish they'd let their own anger out and quit using me!

Michelle came from a home where anger was repressed. Even voices were raised in enthusiasm or intensity was considered anger. Both verbal and nonverbal expressions were given the label of anger.

> I became the great pretender. I should have gone into theater work. I wore this pleasant mask that fooled everyone—except my body. Stuffing all the anger over the years and learning to smile instead made me feel like a fractured personality. In time my body rebelled. I can't stuff much of anything any more, since I lost half of my stomach. I guess my stomach kept score of all the hurts and frustrations. I don't like to smile much any more either. It reminds me too much of living a lie; I wish my parents knew the result of their repression.

Kay was in her 20s, single and struggling with being an adult daughter of an overprotective, worrisome mother.

> My mother has the market cornered on worry. She thinks up things to worry about and calls me every day. I swear she goes over the same things each time, but she has to check up on me to see if I listened to her the day before. I think she creates a checklist of questions to ask. I've told her I'm 27 years old and have been on my own for years, but it doesn't register. She was born a checker-upper, and I guess she'll always be one. I used to work for a person like that, but in time I said, "Enough of this," and I quit. But I can't quit being her daughter, and I don't want to her upset with me either. I want her to be happy with me, but try as hard as I do, I can't seem to really please her. I don't want her angry at me, but I'm getting more and more angry with her!

Many women, like Kay, have had to deal with a controlling person on a regular basis, and it feeds their anger.

Bobbie Reed calls controllers "me only" people. They only want to please themselves all the time and at the expense of others. They are highly critical, but they are oblivious to the criticism of others.[2] They convey their underlying anger through control. Controllers have various tactics, including the following:

- *Indebtedness* ("If it weren't for the good words I put in for you, you'd still be stuck in that pathetic job.")
- *Sarcasm* ("Oh, sure, you remembered about the party. Then how come you arrived here looking so sloppy?")
- *Assumed agreement* ("If you'd stop to think, you'd see I'm right. An alert person could see this right away.")
- *Forced choice* ("Tell me which day you're coming over this week. I'd like to know now.")
- *Judgment statements* ("At 33, you really shouldn't let your mother run your life like that.")
- *Disclaimers* ("I don't mean to be critical, but . . .")
- *Embedded criticism* ("You aren't actually going to wear that to church, are you?")
- *Blame-shifting* ("It doesn't bother me that you're not going to attend, but I think it is going to bother management" [or your mother, or your father, or your friends])
- *Implied double-messages* ("Why should I mind that you call your old mother every day?")
- *Pretending to be talking about themselves while making it clear they're talking about you.* ("I should have known better than to loan you that camera. It's my fault for letting you use it and now it's gone forever.")[3]

The way family members get back at controllers is covert, an underground, indirect response. They often sulk, pout or give the silent treatment. Other retaliatory tactics include withholding sex, talking behind the controller's back, spreading rumors, bungling tasks, making messes, accidentally losing materials or purposely being late. These are passive-aggressive tactics. These expressions of anger are stressful because the fear of being confronted over these behaviors is ever present.

However, if you respond to controllers by rebelling against them, you fall into a different trap: that of becoming just like them. You may express your irritation and frustration through criticism, barbs and even character assassination. Your tactics are obvious, and nothing can dissuade you because you believe the controller deserves everything you dish out. Some people rebel only in their mind and imagination; others let it all out. Guess who ends up looking like the villain?[4]

Fathers and Daughters

Daughters of dominating, angry fathers develop a firm determination to live their lives in a way exactly opposite to what their fathers believed or stood for. They think that in so doing they will show their fathers that they won't be controlled. But what their angry, negative reaction really shows is that these women are still being controlled by their fathers. No wonder their anger doesn't recede.

Sometimes a father controls by becoming demandingly dependent on his daughter. He exaggerates his need to control his daughter, and the daughter becomes increasingly angry at him. Eventually she makes herself less available to be used, but now her guilt directs the anger back against herself.

Perhaps one of the worst scenarios for many women is to be dominated by fear because of a father who is addicted to power and control. This type of father believes he owns those around him. He conveys the message: "I'm your father, and I'm more important than anyone else in your life. Meet my needs!"

A controlling father is quite skilled in using anger to control and manipulate those around him. He tends to hold high and unrealistic expectations for others and is known as a nitpicker. He creates fun at others' expense, often resorting to put-downs and sarcasm. He rarely apologizes and is skilled at making excuses for his mistakes. He projects blame on others, and few dare to disagree with him. No matter what he does, he must come out on top. He must win. Everything in the family must be geared around him. He keeps everybody else on eggshells.

The anger of many dominated daughters often hardens into a cold aloofness toward all other men or into an attitude of defiance toward their fathers and every other man.

Dominated daughters look for men who are loving, warm, sensitive, patient and accepting. But where are they? Usually these women end up attracting men like their fathers or men who have the characteristics they are seeking but who seem weak in comparison. They react to both with angry rebellion.

Mothers and Daughters

Most mother-daughter relationships are characterized by ambivalence. When you hear the word "mother," what do you feel? Many women respond with "Oh, I love my mother. She's the best." And yet in the next breath they move from love to blaming her for what's wrong in their lives. Have you ever felt like making these statements?

- "She's never really understood me."
- "She has never approved of any man I've dated."
- "No matter what subject we talk about, she still tries to run my life."
- "I wish she had paid more attention to me."
- "I wish she had paid less attention to me."
- "I wish she hadn't pushed me so hard."
- "I wish she had pushed me more."

Women are possessive of their mothers and yet are angry at them. They want the approval of their mothers, yet are angry at them. Mothers and daughters can have a wonderful fulfilling relationship one day and be at painful odds the next. It's difficult to have such conflicting feelings.

The anger you feel toward your mother may exist because of unfilled expectations for her that you carry, or because of the cultural idealization we have that mothers are and need to be perfect. Your anger toward your mother could be based on your need for her approval. When it isn't forthcoming or isn't as much as you want, anger protects you—but it also causes you to feel worse about yourself.

Perhaps part of the purpose of any anger you feel toward your mother is to protect you or help you overcome your feelings of powerlessness.

Often anger is a cry of "I don't want this situation to continue. I want it to be different."

But as you know, anger is one step that must lead to another, because it doesn't usually change another person, nor does it prevent a repeat of what you didn't like. Anger increases the distance between two people. It is imperative that you move beyond the anger you feel toward your mother, because women tend to feel much more guilty about being angry than men ever do. When the guilt settles in, it generates still more anger toward your mother, since she's the reason for your guilt in the first place (or so you think).

I find that many women put themselves at the mercy of their mothers by basing their self-esteem and self-approval on them. That intensifies the daughters' needs for any morsels their mothers can give, and it reinforces their beliefs (true or false) that their mothers disapprove of them. That leads to anger, criticism of their mothers and unfulfilling interactions with them—in short, a vicious cycle.

Do you have any fears about your mother? Since fear is one of the major contributors to anger, identifying a woman's mother-fears may help heal the problem so that it's not passed on from generation to generation. Three significant mother-fears are (1) the fear a woman has of losing her mother's love, (2) the fear a woman has of her mother dying, and (3) the fear of becoming like her mother and doing what she has done.

Are you angry with your mother? Take heart: Some resolution is possible.

Numerous women struggling with a mixture of feelings toward their mothers end up feeling sad because their own mothers will never match the image they have for them and because of the emotional distance that separates them from their mothers. When anger and sadness become too intense, emotional numbness and even alienation can set in. You create a wall to keep your mother out, but it keeps you locked up too. That wall also locks in your love. If your anger is not resolved, it may find its release in hostility toward a friend, your husband or your own children, and thus the legacy is continued.

Are you angry with your mother? Take heart: Some resolution is possible. You can learn to lower your expectations for your mother, identify her strengths, accept her faults (and even give her permission to have them) and disconnect your excessive need for her approval. All of this will lessen your anger.

What Can You Do About Your Anger?

What can you do if you've recognized yourself in these descriptions? Where will you go with your anger? How can you change? Let's consider a few practical steps.

Refuse to Dwell on Regrets

Regret is common. I hear these statements constantly:

- "If only Mom or Dad had been different . . ."
- "If only I had learned . . ."
- "If only I hadn't cut loose on her we would still . . ."
- "If only I had said . . ."

By dwelling on these thoughts, you remain encumbered by the past and your future is limited. If there was something you did or didn't do that was a sin, confess it once as stated in 1 John 1:9, "If we . . . admit that we have sinned and confess our sins, he is faithful and just . . . and will forgive our sins and continuously cleanse us from all unrighteousness [everything not in conformity to his will in purpose, thought and action]" (*AMP*).

Then start living your life as though past failures are done with. After all, that's the way God looks at it. Give God your past and see who you can be in the future.

Refuse to Dwell on Recrimination

Harboring thoughts of recrimination is another ineffective way to deal with the past. You are restricting your future when you blame someone for what happened yesterday. We all have a past. How it affects us as adults is our choice.

Refuse to Bank on Renunciation

Renunciation is another common response to the past. We promise to change and do things differently. But past behaviors and attitudes are simply renounced. They are not confronted and cleansed. Lloyd Ogilvie puts this so well:

> We try to close the door on what has been, but all we do is suppress the dragons of memory. Every so often they rap persistently and want to come out into our consciousness for a dress rehearsal in preparation for a rerun in a new situation or circumstance. Renunciation of our memories sounds so very pious. The only things wrong with it is that it doesn't work.[5]

Reflect on the Beliefs You Have Concerning Anger

Look back to some of your answers to the questions listed earlier in this chapter. Use those to help you identify two important concerns: how anger has hurt you in the past and how you want to be different in the future. In order to make this happen, look at the beliefs you have concerning anger—your anger, your father's or mother's anger, or anyone else's—that are still having an impact on your life.

Consider the Decisions You Have Made in the Past That Might Be Negatively Affecting Your Life Now

Many men and women have made decisions in their life based on false beliefs. Those decisions keep them stuck right where they are and even perpetuate their problem with their own or another's anger. Perhaps it would help to ask yourself, *What decisions have I made over the years that are affecting my life in a limiting new way?* You may be surprised at what you discover.

Let People Who Have Hurt You Off the Hook

The next step can best be illustrated by an activity my wife and I enjoy—

trout fishing. We release most of the fish we catch. When a fish comes up close to us, we reach down and let it off the hook. Sometimes it takes the fish a few seconds to discover it has been released. Then it takes advantage of its freedom to dart away and move on with its life.

Letting someone off the hook means letting positive experiences have precedence over negative ones.

Well, it's the same with us if we're going to move on. We need to let other people who hurt us and ourselves off the hook. There's just no other way. We cannot make others or ourselves pay for our sins and mistakes. Letting someone off the hook means being able to reflect on your past and see how it has contributed to the present. It means letting positive experiences have precedence over negative ones.

Think Through What You Want out of the Role of Anger in Your Life

Once you have let the persons who have hurt you off the hook, turn your focus on what you want out of the emotion of anger in your life. Sounds strange, doesn't it, to rationally decide what to do with anger? But think about these questions for a moment:

- What do you want to believe about anger?
- What do you want to feel about anger?
- How do you want to respond and react to the anger of others?
- How do you want to be free from the anger of others?
- How do you want to express your anger in a positive, constructive way?

When you have answered these questions, you will have established your goal and you will have become a future thinker. That's positive. You are developing and drawing toward a vision for your life. When that happens, something dramatic will take place in your mind—you will begin to think of the impossible as possible.

Write a Letter to God Concerning All These Matters

The last step is not what you might expect. It's a letter, a prayer—a vision-ary prayer. I'd like you to write a letter to God telling him about the next years of your life and how, with his strength and guidance, anger will have a different impact and a different place in your life. Take the time to do this. Read it out loud, not just once, but each week.

Anger doesn't have to be the enemy. You can let it be one, or you can make it your ally. It's your choice.

Take Action

1. Return to chapter 1 and note how you answered questions 20 to 23.
2. Is there any way that your family of origin's anger pattern has continued in your family life at this time?
3. How would you like to express anger now?

CHAPTER 12

ANGER IN YOUR MARRIAGE

Gary J. Oliver

Kirk and Paula had been married only six months when she called my office asking for an appointment. After only a few minutes on the phone it became clear that they were beginning to make some of the uncomfortable discoveries that all couples make the first year of marriage.

"I don't understand how he could change in such a short time," Paula exclaimed. "While we were dating Kirk talked a lot and seemed to enjoy being with friends. But since we've been married he has clammed up. He acts like he's taken a course from the Marcel Marceau school of communication." Her humor provided a thin veil for the confusion, hurt and frustration she felt, not to mention the anger she was afraid to admit.

When they came in for the first session Kirk, as you might guess, painted a much different picture. "I'm with people all day and I look forward to coming home and just being with Paula." Kirk continued, "It seems that if we're not talking all of the time something is drastically wrong."

Not only were they having serious disagreements about the quantity of their communication, but they were also going head-to-head over where to live. Before they were married, they had decided that after the wedding Paula would move into Kirk's apartment and they would begin to save money to purchase a home.

However, three months into the marriage Kirk's accountant informed him that it would be financially in their best interest to purchase a home. Kirk had looked around and found several of what he considered to be dream homes. However, each time he showed one to Paula, she invariably found several things wrong with it.

"Before we got married I never dreamed that we'd have arguments over such seemingly little things," Paula said. "It all seemed so much easier when we were just dating." I responded by saying, "That's because it *was* easier." I assured Kirk and Paula that they were not unique in the problems they were facing.

The marriage that they thought had been made in heaven had become anything but heavenly. Unmet needs, unfulfilled expectations and unrealized dreams had increased their disappointment with the relationship. Add a few misunderstandings and some miscommunication and they had the perfect recipe for irritation, frustration and anger.

Like many couples, anger was an emotion that Kirk and Paula knew little about. They saw their disagreement as abnormal and unhealthy. What they didn't know was that they were in the process of taking one of the first steps on the road to developing an intimate relationship. All they could see was that something was wrong, it didn't feel good and they wanted it to stop.

The Inevitability of Anger in a Marriage

Kirk and Paul had bought into one of the most devastating myths about marriage, one that cripples many relationships. They believed that when two people are really in love with each other, they will have few disagreements and virtually no conflict or anger.

I've talked with many people who really believe that healthy couples don't have conflict or get angry. Now it is true that mannequins don't have conflict. It's also true that cadavers don't get angry. But real people in real relationships who are actively working towards figuring out what it means to become one while remaining an individual—they experience disagreement, conflict and anger.

Learning to handle disagreement, conflict and anger is a key part of the process of becoming one. Disagreements in a relationship are inevitable and a fundamental part of achieving intimacy.

To become intimate you have to risk revealing yourself—not just your public self that has been trained how to be acceptable, but also your private self with the weaknesses, flaws, inadequacies and fears of failure and rejection. To become intimate you have to risk letting the other person know how much you need him and how important he is to you. As you become more vulnerable, the risks increase. As the risks increase, the fears increase. As the stakes rise, anger won't be far behind.

The Purifying Process of Disagreement

The process of achieving intimacy is similar to the way that gold was purified in Christ's time. The goldsmith started out with raw gold that contained alloys and impurities. He would put the gold in a container and heat it up. When the gold had melted and had reached just the right temperature, some of the alloys would come to the surface and he would scoop them off.

He would continue this process six more times. At the end, if he had done his job well, he would have pure gold. Each time he would have to heat the gold to just the right temperature. If it wasn't hot enough, the impurities wouldn't come to the surface. If it got too hot, he would lose some of the precious metal.

Our relationships are a lot like gold. They start out in a very rough form. We have a very crude idea of what it means to love. We want intimacy but aren't always sure what it is and what is involved in achieving it. However, God knows all about intimacy. He allows differences, difficulties and disagreements to enter into our relationships and they tend to heat things up.

As the relationships get hotter our personal alloys and impurities, such as pride, jealousy, selfishness, resentment, insecurity and fear, are brought to the surface, identified and removed. With each new conflict the gold of our relationship becomes a bit purer. If we keep things in

God's hands and allow the process to continue, we will end up with a relationship that's pure gold. But it's not easy and it doesn't happen overnight.

God wants to teach us how to use our anger to help bring the alloys and impurities of our lives to the surface. The healthy expression of our anger can help us clarify, understand and appreciate our differences. When we deny our anger and run from conflict we are running from the very process that God can use to heal our hurts and knit our hearts more tightly together in love.

Healthy Anger and Strong Marriages

The greater our love for someone, the greater our capacity to experience a wide range of emotions in connection with that person. Those emotions include irritation, resentment, anger and even rage. That is true whether we're dealing with our own parents, our spouse or our children.

The people to whom we give the most time and energy and in whom we invest the greatest amount of love and other emotions are the ones we have the highest expectations of. They are also the ones with the greatest potential to trigger in us such emotions as fear, hurt, frustration and eventually anger. The late Dr. David Mace, a pioneer in the marriage enrichment movement, is quoted as saying, "Marriage and family living generate in normal people more anger than people experience in any other social situation."[1]

Anger is not necessarily a sign of relational immaturity or instability. Anger is an inherent component of all human relationships. But it is especially prevalent in romantic ones. The

The more dependent on and vulnerable to someone you are, the more likely he or she will be the object of your hostility as well as your affection.

more dependent on and vulnerable to someone you are, the more likely he or she will be the object of your hostility as well as your affection.

People in healthy relationships argue and disagree. The difference is that their disagreements result in increased understanding, trust and security. They reflect a mutual respect.

Healthy expression of anger is a testimony to the strength of a marriage. Relationships that don't acknowledge or express anger are usually fragile, unstable and anemic. For anger not to be expressed suggests that the couple isn't secure enough or that the marriage isn't strong enough to handle disagreement. Moreover, "when anger is denied or avoided, then honesty and trust are compromised and communication is constrained as one or both partners use energy to hide their anger."[2]

Given the inevitability of anger in all relationships, the question is not whether to express it, but how and when. The long-term success of a relationship depends on your willingness to find healthy ways for expressing and dealing with each other's anger.

Trigger Points for Anger in a Marriage

We asked the women we surveyed to tell us what they saw as the things that sparked anger in a marriage. Some of that they said is given below.

The faults men have. When we asked women, "Where does the anger in a marriage come from?" what do you suppose the number one response of women was? You guessed it—men. And not just men in general but specific and not-so-enduring qualities of certain men. These are some of the characteristics the women in our survey listed:

They don't listen
They are controlling
They fear intimacy
They aren't nurturing
They are selfish
They don't know how to communicate
They are arrogant
They think just being there is enough
They never apologize
They are too concrete

They are deceptive
They demand love-making without loving
They are inconsiderate
They have to be asked to do anything
They take us for granted
They only care about the bottom line
They don't look us in the eye
They make jokes when we need to be serious

Could you have contributed any of these? What isn't on the list that you think should be added?

Psychotherapist Nancy Good in her book *How to Live with the Difficult Man You Love* identifies the more common ways men make women angry in relationships.

He misunderstands you.
He doesn't hear, doesn't respond to you.
He criticizes in a destructive manner.
He betrays you.
He mocks you, makes fun of you.
He tries to control you.
He ignores what needs to be done.
He exhibits explosive, possibly violent behavior.
He gives you the silent treatment.
He blames you when things to wrong.
He is nasty in general.
He messes up what you ask.
He is chronically unenthusiastic.[3]

Children. In our survey, the number four cause for anger was children. The demands of children increase a couple's vulnerability to experiencing anger, not only at them, but also at each other. Nancy Samalin expresses what many of the women in our survey have experienced.

For many families, home is a battleground, filled with constant
bickering, shouting matches, and exhausting power struggles. . . .
Parents are amazed that they can go from relative calm to utter frustration in a few seconds. An uneaten egg or spilled juice at breakfast
can turn a calm morning into a free-for-all. In spite of parents' best
intentions, bedtime becomes wartime, meals end with children in
tears and food barely touched, and car rides deteriorate into stress-
filled shouting matches . . . I never even knew I had a temper until
I had children. It was very frightening that these children I loved so
much, for whom I had sacrificed so much, could arouse such
intense feelings of rage in me, their mother, whose primary responsibility was to nurture and protect them.[4]

A lack of understanding of basic differences in personality. When Kirk and
Paula were dating, each was taken with the uniqueness of the beloved
and by dreams of what life would be like together; they didn't take time
to note and understand some of their important differences. They loved
what felt good and they ignored or minimized what didn't.

If their premarital counseling had included exposure to a tool such as
the Myers-Briggs Type Indicator, they would have understood that Kirk
was an introvert and Paula was an extrovert. While Kirk enjoyed being
with people, he also valued his "alone time." Too much "people time"
drained him. He needed alone time to recharge his battery. After working
and talking all day, he looked forward to coming home and just "being
there" with Paula. Can you imagine how painful it was for Kirk to feel con-
demned and rejected by the woman he loved—simply for being himself?

As an extrovert, Paula not only enjoyed being with people but she was
also energized by them. Paula could work and talk all day, come home
exhausted and want to have a few friends over to help her get picked back
up again. What was exhausting for Kirk was energizing for Paula. What
was energizing for Kirk was exhausting (and boring) to Paula.

Paula was correct in her recollection that Kirk seemed much more
outgoing when they were dating. The process of dating and getting
acquainted is a much more extroverted process. Paula had never seen
what Kirk was like behind closed doors. She hadn't even considered the

possibility that Kirk might need to "shut down." On the other hand Kirk never dreamed that Paula would want to talk "nonstop all of the time." He assumed that when they weren't together she would recharge her batteries the same way he did. That's a common mistake many people make. We often assume that other people are, or should be, the way we are. If they aren't like we are, then they must be wrong.

Was either Kirk or Paula wrong? Of course not. They were simply different. "Different" is not a dirty word. Differences are what provide depth and breadth to a relationship. Our differences can turn a black and white relationship into living color. Unfortunately, they hadn't identified and didn't understand some of their most basic differences.

When we haven't identified and don't understanding our differences, it is easy for them to catch us off guard. They can make us feel uncomfortable, challenge the perceived "rightness" of our perspective and force us to reevaluate our opinions and ways of doing things.

A lack of understanding of gender differences and appreciation for them. In past years there have been tremendous efforts on the part of some to convince the public that there are no substantive differences between men and women. Any of what might appear to be differences are simply superficial cosmetic differences caused by our society.

We disagree with that conclusion. Our research, our examination of the clear teaching of Scripture and the experience of the women we have worked with cause us to conclude that, while

> *Scripture teaches us that while men and women are of equal intelligence, giftedness, significance, value and worth, they are also different from one another.*

men and women are of equal intelligence, giftedness, significance, value and worth, they are also different from one another. Being equal doesn't mean that we are the same.[5]

In terms of the marriage relationship one of the most important ways in which men and women differ relates to their communication styles. Deborah Tannen notes in *You Just Don't Understand: Women and Men in Conversation* that many of the conflicts between men and women are caused by basic misunderstandings of the opposite sex. For example, while driving in the car a woman asked her husband, "Would you like to stop for ice cream?" Her husband thought about it for a minute and said, "No." Later on he became frustrated because he realized that his wife was annoyed. Why? Because she had wanted to stop. "If you wanted to stop why didn't you just say so?" he asked.[6]

Both had misread the other. She had incorrectly taken her husband's "no" as nonnegotiable and irreversible. The husband had misconstrued his wife's question as a request for a decision rather than the beginning of a discussion about what both of them would like. Many men are more comfortable giving a one-word decision such as "yes" or "no" rather than entering into a discussion whose direction is unclear.

Many men and women differ in their ways of coping with problems. When many women talk about problems they are seeking understanding and sympathy and not trying to find "the solution." They want to share their situation with someone they can trust. The support they get from the process of someone's interaction may be more meaningful than getting to the answer.

Since many men don't talk about problems unless they want advice, they often frustrate women by offering advice and trying to solve the problem rather than taking the time trying to understand it. They are much more likely to move to the "bottom line." They think they are loving their wives by giving them the solution to the problem. They are often caught off guard and surprised when their wife doesn't seem to appreciate that response.

When in the course of a conversation a man discovers that a male friend has a personal problem, he is likely to change the subject out of his respect for the other's need for independence. Many men assume that the extended discussion of a problem will be awkward and make it even more serious and thus cause the other man to feel worse. Women are just the opposite. When a friend shares a problem with them, they are much more likely to show respect and concern by responding with active listening, inviting more information and asking pertinent questions.

When it comes to giving feedback, women are more likely to look at one another directly while men often fail to maintain direct eye contact. Women are more likely to ask questions when involved in a conversation. To show they care about the person they are listening to and tracking the conversation they may offer small cues like "uh-huh," "that's right" or "yeah." When a woman says "yeah," that suggests that she is following what you're saying. Most men will say "yeah" only when they agree with you. Overall men give fewer signals than women and are more likely to respond with blanket statements and challenges.

Another difference that is a major source of hurt and anger to many women involves making apologies. Many women say "I'm sorry" as a way of making a connection and joining with the other person. It can be another way of saying "I'm sorry this happened to you" or "I'm sorry you feel so bad—I do too." For many men saying "I'm sorry" means admitting that they were wrong and they need to make an apology. They believe this puts them in a one-down position and for many men that is unmasculine and unacceptable.

One final difference is the way in which men and women deal with conflict. In an interview, Dr. John Gottman stated that in a marriage,

Women tend to see it as their responsibility to do something about it. Men tend to withdraw—they'll work harder, do things with friends instead of family. It's important for couples to understand this so they don't attribute problems to one another when the problems really have to do with gender differences.[7]

Steps for Dealing with Conflict

It's an occupational hazard of being married to experience anger. Anger often leads to conflict and conflict can be a key to healthier, stronger and more intimate relationships. Since dealing with anger and working through conflict have such potential for building trust and intimacy in a relationship, what are some specific ways in which we can more effectively deal with anger and conflict in marriage and make them work for us rather than against us?

Develop Good Communication Skills

The first step is to work on decreasing unhealthy anger and unnecessary conflict. Since much of the anger and conflict in marriage is due to miscommunication, you can significantly reduce the number of unnecessary conflicts by actively working on developing good communication skills. This is actually easier than it might appear.

One of the best places to start is to read together a basic book on effective couple communication. As Kirk and Paula went through the book *Communication: Key to Your Marriage,* by my coauthor, they were amazed to see what a difference the practical insights made in their communication. Both of them had been so focused on getting the other person to understand their point of view neither one was spending much time listening. They had fallen into the very common trap of trying to solve problems they didn't understand and trying to understand problems they hadn't defined.

Keep Short Accounts

It didn't take Kirk and Paula long to learn that in marriage it is easy to collect fears and hurts and frustrations and put them in cold storage until you have a full load—and then "Pow!" When they tried to go back and figure out what caused the problem, they had no idea why they were arguing or what they were even so upset about. In fact they would often find themselves arguing about what they thought they had been arguing about.

Much of the anger in Kirk and Paula's marriage was over small issues that were either unidentified or were identified but not dealt with. Over time and with many repetitions these micro issues became what appeared to be large issues that were threatening and seemed impossible to deal with.

These kinds of situations remind me of hot air balloons. From a distance they look small, but the closer you get, the bigger you see they are. Yet once you remove the hot air they become comparatively small and manageable. Many of the issues separating Kirk and Paula were long on hot air and short on substance.

When you become aware of a conflict try to define the problem. What's the issue? How long has it been a problem? Whose problem is it? Is it really that big a deal? There are times when we need to learn how to draw a line between issues that need to be confronted and frustrations that are a normal part of living with someone else.

Develop a Sense of Perspective

Much of the anger in marriage can be traced to personal idiosyncrasies, minor annoyances or passing irritations. Cindy and Roger have been married for over 20 years. She said that for the first 7 years of their marriage she would fuss and fume at him for a variety of behaviors that she found frustrating.

Finally at the encouragement of a friend, Cindy went to see a counselor "to find some ways to help Roger change." Her therapist challenged her

At times we need to learn how to distinguish between issues that need to be confronted and frustrations that are a normal part of living with someone else.

to, for a two-week period, make a list of all of the terrible, awful and horrible things he did. As she read through her list, Cindy told me "I was amazed and a bit embarrassed at what I discovered." Her list looked like this:

He is cheery and talkative when he gets up in the morning. He likes his toast well done, almost burnt, and he makes a lot of noise when he bites into it. He fondles the remote control for the TV and likes to watch several shows at a time. He doesn't close the sliding glass closet doors after he gets dressed in the morning. Sometimes when he laughs he will snort. He makes a weird sound when he clears his throat. He refills the ice-cube trays too high, and the water spills over and makes puddles of

ice in the freezer. When he goes shopping for clothes, he has a
hard time making up his mind.

When she saw how small and insignificant these issues were she decided, "All things considered, Roger wasn't that bad, and that I was a selfish
and immature first-class crab to let those little irritations bother me."

When you choose to express your anger, draw a line between the differences that demand confrontation and those that are simply a part of
living with someone else. Before you allow an issue to consume too
much of your time ask yourself, *How important is this?* Is it a low-ticket or
a high-ticket item? On a scale of 1 to 10 a low-ticket item would score
1 through 5. A low-ticket item is something that may irritate or frustrate
you but it really isn't a big deal. All of the things on Cindy's list were
clearly low-ticket items.

A high-ticket item would rate 6 to 10. High-ticket items would
include issues such as how affection is expressed, how important decisions are made, who decides where we spend your vacations, how
finances are allocated and, one of Kirk and Paula's favorite issues, where
you will live.

Acknowledge Your Own Contribution to the Problem

Let's assume you've decided that the issue is one that you need to
address. Before you spend too much time looking at all the things your
spouse needs to change, ask yourself, *What is my part of the problem?* It is
much easier for us to pick up a magnifying glass than it is to pick up a
mirror. It's much easier to pray, "Lord, change my husband, children,
friends" than it is to pray "Lord, change me!" In Psalm 139:23-24 David
writes, "Search me, O God, and know my heart; Try me and know my
anxious thoughts; And see if there be any hurtful way in me, And lead
me in the everlasting way" (*NASB*).

Be Clear About the Source of Your Anger

Ask yourself, *Is this about my husband, my children—or is it in response to a combination of things from the day?* Women may have a tendency to direct their
global anger toward their husband. "Sometimes I'll come home incensed

at how a few of the men at work have treated me," wrote Lois, "and it's almost as if I'm looking for my husband to make one wrong move so that I can pounce on him and thus in a crazy kind of way 'get back' at the other men. I know it's unfair and irrational."

Of course women aren't the only ones who tend to do this. It seems to be the nature of human nature to suppress and hide some of our fears, hurts and frustrations and then let them out on the people we care about and love the most.

Practice Constructive Criticism

If the issue is a legitimate high-ticket item, practice constructive criticism. The best place to start is by getting the facts. Develop the invaluable skill of asking clarifying questions. Questions can decrease the intensity of the moment, broaden your perspective, encourage new ways of thinking, stimulate the need for gathering more facts and help you see the value of looking at as more options.

Remember that confrontation is usually most effective when it takes the form of a rational, clearly reasoned discussion, not a loud tirade, a brutal put-down or a devastating downpour of tears. Once again let me emphasize that if you feel on the verge of losing control, take a brief time out to clear your mind and regain your focus. Take a few deep breaths or step outside and go for a walk. Pray. Remind yourself of some of God's promises and of the indwelling presence of the Holy Spirit in your life. Remember that you're never alone.

Rehearse Your Confrontation

Ask yourself if it would help for you to rehearse what you are going to say in order to have a constructive confrontation. Here are some suggestions:

- Rehearse with the Lord in prayer your confrontation. First pray silently and then out loud.
- You can use the empty chair technique. Place two chairs opposite each other. You sit in one chair and pretend your spouse is in the other chair. Tell the empty chair what you are feeling and why.

• You can write a letter to your spouse that you will never mail. After you have read the letter out loud two or three times you may be surprised at how much more confident and clear you are.

When you begin a confrontation, be sure to address your spouse by name. Give him specific information about your concerns with one or two examples. Try to avoid coming across as too negative or critical. Let him know how his behavior has affected you and how you feel about it.

If you are angry, explain that you are angry and give specific reasons for your anger. Then let him know what you would like to see happen in the future. Make it clear that your main concern is a stronger and healthier relationship.

At the end of the conversation, thank him for taking the time to listen; and then, if he is a Christian, ask if you could pray together. Then never bring up the situation again.

Many of the women in our survey said that expressing angry feelings is an uncomfortable task. Remember that asserting yourself is not an act of aggression. It is an act of communication. It is saying *I value myself, you and this relationship enough to speak the truth in love.*

Take Action

1. What does the anger in your marriage stem from? What positive steps can you take to resolve the problem?
2. What angers you the most in dealing with your children? What positive steps can you take to resolve the problem?
3. What frustrates you the most about you and your partner's similarities and differences? What positive steps can you take to resolve the problem?

CHAPTER 13

OVERREACTIONS AND UNDERREACTIONS

H. Norman Wright

Do you feel good about the way you express your anger? Do you misuse it toward yourself or toward others? Are you wondering what to do with your anger? Let's consider some of the more typical ways anger is misused and what you can do about it.

Overreaction

At times do you get angry at something insignificant, and even though you are aware of it you seem unable to do anything about it? Often women who react this way are slow to even recognize their anger and its buildup. Often the anger builds up over a period of days, weeks and even months; then something minor happens at home or at work and there's an explosion. Overreacting people are usually reacting to the past rather than to what's going on in the present. That is something to keep in mind. (You might even put in writing and post it where you can see it easily.)

If you tend to overrespond with your anger, try this: At the end of each day for a week or two, inventory the times that you may have been annoyed or irritated. What drew forth an angry response from you? Were there any times when you anticipated a problem with a family member or someone at work? Did you experience anger at any time over something you thought might happen but never materialized?

As you look over your inventory, determine how you might deal with such situations in the future. What could you say or do each time you feel irritated, in order to handle the emotion immediately and not let it build? And when you think about the people who made you angry, don't just assume that what they said or did was intentional. Ask some clarifying questions. You may discover that there was nothing intentional in their behavior or that they weren't even aware that what they did or said was a problem.

Lost Opportunities

Cindy expressed yet another common difficulty with anger. "You know," she said, "there are times when I wonder if I'm angry and don't even know it. Sometimes I get angry, but it seems to take so long to arrive. Rarely does it come when the problem occurs. It's like I have a delayed fuse, and sometimes I don't even know that it's lit until I get angry. It's hard for me to experience anger. And I wish it would happen at the time I need it the most."

Like Cindy, many women regret lost opportunities to express their anger. Later on they can imagine what they would have liked to have said. They have the feeling that it might have been beneficial to have become angry at the time. Often the difficulty is that a slow anger responder isn't used to expressing anger in the presence of other people, or chooses not to. In order to feel her anger, she may need privacy.

If you are like Cindy, schedule some private time so you can reflect on situations that happened during the day. Were there any incidents that might have triggered an angry response in you but didn't? What were your thoughts at that time, negative or positive? Were the other people fair at the time of the incident? When did you first become aware of your anger? What did you want to do or say at that time but didn't?

As you think about each incident, take your emotional temperature to determine if you are angry. If you *are* angry, ask yourself, *What do I want to have happen when I express my anger?* Then express your feelings right away, in private. Doing this immediately can be healthy for your relationships and prevent a buildup that will be expressed sooner or later.

Guilt

Carol expressed a unique conflict over her anger. "It isn't just when I express anger that I feel anger," she confided. "It's when I feel anger that the guilt starts. I end up feeling miserable over the fact that I get angry. My guilt cripples my anger and keeps it from being productive. Perhaps I'm expecting that I should be more in control of my feelings. I wish I could control my guilt rather than have it control my anger."

Carol and others like her can learn to eliminate their guilt. It's important first of all to identify where the beliefs you have about your anger came from and whether they're accurate or not. Often our beliefs and values come into play and generate the guilt we feel. Make a list of the times when you either felt or expressed anger and what it was about. Determine whether your

> *Each day give yourself permission to feel anger, but don't express it. By making the choice not to express your anger you show that you are in control of it.*

anger was justified or not. Formulate a statement that you will say to your guilt the next time it occurs. Give yourself permission to become angry when anger is needed.

If you still tend to feel guilty, list three reasons for believing your anger is wrong and then three reasons for believing it's right. Each day give yourself permission to feel anger, but don't express it. By making the choice not to express your anger you will be showing that you are in control of it. Tell yourself that feeling anger is nothing to feel guilty about. Make a chart and keep track of the level of your guilt for one month to identify your progress. Develop a plan and a method for expressing anger in a way that you feel positive about.

Anger That Hurts Others

Colleen told me, "When I'm angry, you know it. So do the people who've upset me. I don't edit. I cut loose, and I don't care how they feel. If they're hurt or put down, well, they deserved it after what they did or said to me."

Anger that hurts others is a problem. And not everyone is as unconcerned as Colleen. Many realize that their relationships with family, work associates and friends are deteriorating because of their overly direct anger attacks. Also, too often their anger attacks are directed at the other person's character rather than what he or she did, which means their anger is seen not as anger but as aggression. Five steps can help you change this pattern.

- Think back over a time when you were overly angry with someone. Don't give any regard to what he or she said or did. Think about what you said, what you did, your nonverbals and your gestures. Imagine that you were the other person. How might you have felt receiving your anger?
- Select two of your anger encounters and write down what you could have said to make each a constructive vent. Focus on what the other person did and what you would have preferred him or her to do. Imagine yourself telling this person *only* what he or she did that was unacceptable, why you didn't like it and what you would have preferred.
- Notice how this new approach made you feel—about yourself, the person and your response. Was it a better feeling than what

you experienced before?
- Apply Ephesians 4:26 and Proverbs 16:32 to your new response. Does it fit?
- Make a commitment to yourself, to God and to one other person as to how you will respond the next time you are angry.

Misdirected Anger

Kathy told me about her pattern of taking out her anger on the wrong person and her tendency to complain about others.

> It's like I'm on an archery range, and every time I shoot I miss the target and hit the target next to it. I was angry at my son the other day, and yet I took it out on his sister. I wasn't even aware that I was angry at him until I exploded, and then I had to deal with the problems my anger created between my daughter and me. This has happened at work as well. I'm often not aware that I'm angry with another coworker, and yet later on I'm griping my head off about him! I guess I am angry but take it out by griping.

The first step in correcting this misuse of anger is to figure out the reason you're reluctant to let out your anger directly at the people you're angry with. Is it their position of power or authority, a fear of their anger or a fear of their rejection? Has this been your usual way of responding over the years? Is this the style you use only with family or coworkers or just certain kids of people? What do you gain by not expressing your anger directly? What do you lose by not confronting directly?

Ask yourself what it would take for you to be willing to express your anger directly to the person who angered you. Commit yourself to do this on the next three occasions when that person makes you angry. When you do confront him or her, you might want to state the underlying reason for your anger (fear, hurt, frustration or whatever), as well as stating what you would prefer the person to do differently in the future.

(These clarifying statements are helpful for changing all the problem responses to anger that we are discussing.)

Preserved Anger

"I'm a keeper," Teri said. "Unfortunately, somewhere over the years I've picked up the idea that anger should never be shared with others. So I've learned to keep it to myself and contain it. Stuff it would be a better word! I guess that's why I'm so thin. My stomach has taken the brunt of my anger. I knew this a long time ago, but I was still willing to put up with it. It seemed a small price to pay for not creating a scene with my anger."

Teri is like many women whose bodies have become a dumping ground for the toxic waste of buried anger. Upset stomach, depression, hypertension and cardiovascular disease, irritable bowel disease and suicide are just a few of the physical symptoms that occur when people absorb their anger. Teri knew about it and was willing to pay the price. Many women don't know about it and still pay the price.

What can you do if you are like Teri? First, if you have a number of physical symptoms as well as unshared anger, consider the possibility of a correlation between your anger and the symptoms. Be sure to discuss this possibility with your family physician and ask him or her to recommend literature on this subject. Keep a written record of your physical symptoms and your anger to see how the two connect. When you become irritated at home or at work—or wherever—keep track of how much time it takes for your body to begin responding to your anger.

Once you have identified the correlation, become aware of your anger sooner each time. Identify the beliefs or experiences that cause you not to express your anger toward another person. Select appropriate healthy responses from this and other chapters and learn to use them instead of stuffing your anger. Practice, rehearse and implement those new steps.

Controlled by Others' Anger

"My problems start when others get angry at me," Linda said. "I get along fine with my family and the others at work—unless someone gets angry at me or lets me know they are displeased in some way. Then watch out. I come on way too strong. Usually the other person is taken aback and confused. It's the other person's anger that I'm responding to in the first place."

Many of us have difficulty responding to others' anger, and our initial response is a defensive posture coupled with the offensive stance of being aggressive. Sometimes we may be feeling that others shouldn't expect us to be perfect. But if we blame their anger for activating our aggression, it could be we are expecting them to be perfect too.

Some steps you can take will help. One is to think about what you're doing. How do you feel about yourself reacting to another person's anger? Do you *want* to become angry? After all, isn't that what you dislike in the other person? There is probably nothing you can do to keep others from becoming angry, so why not give them permission to do so? And when they respond in anger, you can (1) just listen and ask clarification questions; (2) reflect back what you heard them saying and feeling; (3) let them know you want to think over what they've just said for a minute; or (4) tell them you want to hear what they have to say and can understand their being upset at this time. Whatever approach you take, plan and rehearse your new response a number of times.

The Tears of Anger

Something both women and men have expressed frustration over when it occurs in women—crying to express anger. This response is especially confusing to a man. Crying comes in many shapes and sizes. Sometimes it's just the feeling of choking up and not being able to talk. Sometimes it's having your eyes fill with tears. Some persons will avert their eyes or mumble that there's a speck in their eyes as they wipe them. Others simply find the tears pouring forth. You may find it easier to cry in some settings than others. For most people, it is easiest to cry at home and the most difficult to cry at work.

Tears that spring from anger appear to emerge from frustration that what one is saying isn't being heard by another. Such tears may also embody grieving that one's ideas are rejected by another out of hand, before they've been given a fair hearing (literally). They may incorporate fear and anger that the other person does not really want to hear what you're saying.

For some people it is easier to cry than to show their anger. For others the intensity of their anger frustrates them so much that they become tongue-tied. This new frustration, coupled with the initial frustration, leads to tears. Some people give themselves permission to cry but not to show anger, so the anger is channeled into crying. Have you ever heard the expression, "I was reduced to tears"? That is the ultimate sense of frustration.

If this is what you do, here are some suggestions. First, let others know that you tend to cry when you become frustrated or angry, and that in time you will learn to become more direct with your anger. Let them know that you need a bit of time to compose yourself, and then you'll be all right.

As soon as you begin to feel something, listen to it. Immediately after you have cried, analyze what happened, what was said, how you reacted, and what you felt—whether it was anger, fear, hurt, insecurity or frustration. The next time a situation occurs at home or at work and you feel yourself beginning to choke or tear up, excuse yourself and go into another room. Let your tears out and then identify your true feelings at the same time. When you return, don't apologize for your tears, but instead state what you were beginning to feel. Mention that the next time, you might cry or you might be able to come out with your real feelings.

Spend time visualizing how you want to respond with your anger the next time. Imagine yourself saying, "I'm upset over . . ." or "Right now I'm angry . . ." Practicing in advance will make it possible to move from tears to your true feelings.[1]

Chronic Anger

There is one last difficulty that infects many of us—chronic anger. Perhaps you've struggled with this over the years. Or perhaps you've had to live with an individual who is in a state of chronic anger. Either way, you can testify to the major impact people with chronic anger have on those around them.

Chronic anger has been defined as a pattern of thinking, acting and feeling in which the individual actually looks for or prolongs her anger, or both. This pattern is the opposite of the one followed by anger-avoiders. A chronically angry person is often oversensitive to anger cues. It's as though she pays selective attention to them and welcomes the opportunity to react with anger. Her antenna has been programmed to hunt out and respond to any stimulus that will kick off anger. And because she is overly conditioned to the possibility of becoming angry, she underreacts to cues that would lead to her becoming happy, joyful or fearful.

Some people have become much more comfortable with their anger than with sadness or fear.

After she is aware of the factor that can trigger her anger, she moves into the excitement phase, and her mind fixates on the sensations and thoughts that accompany chronic anger. Her anger is activated and concentrated, which lessens her ability to think calmly and clearly about what is taking place. The more she focuses on her anger, the more it builds. A woman with a pattern of chronic anger tends to let anger propel her into impulsive, exaggerated action. When that happens we often say that she is out of control. Often the anger flows into a rage response. Trying to talk a chronically angry person out of her anger does very little except to feed it.

Chronically angry people cannot or will not withdraw from their anger. They tend to brood and dwell on past hurts and slights. Either their anger is on the "high" button or it's on the "simmer" button. There is no relief from their anger, for a chronically angry person never completely lets go of it.[2]

A chronically angry person's interpersonal relationships are poor and her other emotions are stifled because anger crowds them out. What does chronic anger tell us?

Chronic Anger Is a Signal That Something Is Seriously Wrong

Whatever is wrong could be a legitimate concern, but unfortunately the anger itself usually does not tell us what the problem is. If you are a chronically angry person and you feel anger beginning to build, you might find it helpful to say, "I am starting to get angry, but I need to take it slow and discover the message of my anger." Who knows? It could be a false alarm.

Chronic Anger May Be . . .

An attempt to resolve difficult life problems. Using chronic anger as a means of resolving difficult life problems may seem like a good idea, but it is usually counterproductive. Anger distances us from other people rather than drawing them closer. It can actually compound our difficulties. If it seems to solve a problem, it probably hasn't. Other persons have probably been intimidated.

A long-term habit. Habits develop because the person has received some sort of benefit from that behavior. The anger may have had some value in the past; but, unfortunately, now that it has developed into a habit, it has become a leftover without much of a function. It only creates problems. The habit of anger is actually controlling a chronically angry person's life. For people who want to feel like they're in control, that's not a pleasant thought.

A means to control others. Controllers often use anger as a power play. Some believe it is the only way to stay in control or get others activated. This type of anger is usually referred to as "instrumental anger" rather than the emotional state of "expressive anger." Instrumental anger has extremely negative effects within a family situation and can cripple the work environment. It is wielded by a socially defective person. But she usually doesn't like to hear this or admit it.

An attempt to gain status. Some people have learned that they can elicit respect, gain status or draw out admiration when they are willing to risk overpowering others, especially those in a position of authority. They're referred to as "hotheads" or worse, but they don't mind the label. It gets them the attention they want. But in order to maintain the recognition and respect of others, they need to keep looking for reasons to become and stay angry. They can't afford to let up or rest from their anger. Some actually boast about their ability to intimidate. But often inside, especially among older women, there is a deep longing for the softer, positive, loving relationship skills that would cause others to want to be close to them.

A way to maintain physical and emotional distance from others. People who find it difficult to accept closeness and intimacy may use chronic anger as a means of keeping others from getting too close to them. It's as though they are carrying a "no trespassing" sign or a "beware of me, I bite" placard. Intense anger will actually remove people from your life, even though that might not have been your original purpose. Some people want to keep others away only for a while or at certain times, but that isn't the message people hear. They hear, "I want you out of my life forever. Keep on going!"

The glue that holds a relationship together. There are couples who argue from morning to evening. Their relationship is held together by this tension. It's the old phrase "I can't live with you, and I can't live without you." The pain these couples experience and the example their behavior gives to their children is unfortunate. The children learn that intimacy is only obtained through conflict. If one individual started responding without being angry, the relationship would probably collapse; the couple wouldn't know what to do without their anger.

A defense against shame and real or perceived threats to a person's self-esteem. When you feel shame, you also feel deficient, inferior, worthless and useless. The most typical response against an attack on your identity is rage. Each time you're shamed it goes into your storehouse of memories. When the next incident occurs, your reaction is not just to the current situation but also to the memory you have built up. That leads to resentment and a sense of seething bitterness. Your memories keep churning for weeks, months, and in some cases I have seen, even years. The response I have witnessed in counseling is almost as though the inciting incident occurred that very day. Some people who experience rage against shame become batterers. Believing that they have the right to attack because they were attacked first, they believe they are justified in what they are doing.

Self-defense against experiencing other feelings, such as fear, sadness and love. People who use anger this way may not even know that this is what they are doing; nevertheless, they have become much more comfortable with their anger than with sadness or fear. If a person is afraid of the closeness that often accompanies love, anger will soon take care of that problem.

An expression of righteous indignation. Our world has so many problems and injustices that we believe we have the right to be angry. *We should be angry*, we think. Someone has to attack those who hold different and inferior viewpoints. So we justify what we are doing on moral grounds. But we may not be fighting simply for a moral cause, but for the feeling of our own superiority. Sometimes anger of this type seems right and proper, and other times it is way off base. Cynicism and contempt permeate our expressions of anger. Unfortunately, this type of anger tends to work for some people, who override the opposition and appear to win.

A means of making a person feel activated. This last purpose of anger has an almost addictive quality. Because anger contains an abundance of energy it helps some people who ordinarily live a dull and colorless life to become activated, or it gives them the experience of a "high" because of the adrenaline rush. These people look for reasons to become angry and even seek out anger to receive a thrill they would ordinarily never experience otherwise.

Exploring Alternatives to Chronic Anger

Some angry habits you may have, both verbal and nonverbal, could include frowning, glaring, snapping your fingers or hitting your palm against your thigh, yelling, swearing, slamming doors and chopping the vegetables into minute pieces with a knife.[3]

If you have this tendency to anger, answer this question: Do you want to explore the possibility of learning to react in another manner? I'm not asking if you want to change, because you could be experiencing a lot of benefits from your anger (even though there are greater benefits when you learn to moderate your anger), or you may not believe you could possibly change. The first step in dealing with life in a new way is to consider the possibility that there is a different way to respond to the world. As you consider that, think about what you could replace your anger with so that you would have an alternative.

Once you have a picture in your mind of a different way to respond, remember that in moving ahead you are not totally giving up your usual way of responding. You are just shelving it for a while in order to explore another way of handling the causes and purposes of your chronic anger. If the new way doesn't work after extensive attempts or if it doesn't bring you greater benefits, you can always discard it and go back to your previous pattern.

I realize that that is easier said than done, and yet it is possible. Look carefully at the other sections of this book, which give practical steps for changing and implementing new responses. Many people have made the switch; otherwise we would not even be considering the possibility. Keep this thought in mind. If God can see you changing and becoming a different person (and He can), why not grasp His perception of you and make it your own? Begin to think of yourself as a person who is not chronically angry. Create a vision of what you can become rather than what you have been.

Take Action

1. When you express your anger, what is it that you would like to happen?
2. To what degree do you feel guilty when angry?
3. Go back through this chapter and write out your answers to each of the questions asked. Seeing your response in writing will have a significant impact on you.
4. Describe the vision you have for your life concerning anger.

CHAPTER 14

WHAT CAN I DO ABOUT MY ANGER?

Gary J. Oliver

Anna said, "Every time I lose my temper and yell at Tom or the kids I feel like a total failure. I promise the Lord and myself that it will never happen again . . . but it does."

Do you think that Anna is a cream puff, locomotive or steel magnolia? When I share this illustration with women's groups, most guess that Anna is a locomotive. But she's a cream puff—because when a cream puff has been under pressure long enough, she will often "lose it."

Anna, the mother of four children, had been married to Chuck for 14 years. She was a kind and gracious woman, loved by her husband and children and respected by her friends. I was a bit surprised when she told me, in a very calm and soft voice, that she needed help in dealing with her anger.

She told me that she had been raised in a home with an angry father who made it clear that he was the head of the house. "I don't mean head in the healthy and biblical sense of the word," she said emphatically, with a hint of bitterness in her voice. "He ran our home with an iron fist. I promised myself that when I grew up I would not be an angry person like my dad." Anna continued, "I remember dad saying, 'I'm the man and God has made me the head of this house.' Apparently anyone who disagreed with him was questioning God."

So Anna had grown up believing that being a good woman meant being a quiet, submissive, compliant, complacent and anger-free woman. Women, like children, were best seen and not heard. That's what she was told and that's what she saw modeled. "Mom was a kind and gentle woman and I never once heard her disagree with Dad." Whenever she would even get close to disagreeing, Anna's Dad would give her mom "the look" and everyone knew what that meant.

Anna had met Chuck at a Christian college. They dated for two years and were married in his senior year. They had their first child 10 months after their wedding, and in the next four years they had three more children. Due to the birth of their first child, Anna wasn't able to complete her college education.

After Chuck's graduation he went on for his law degree and joined a large law firm. For the first several years he worked long hours, and the family life centered around his schedule and his needs. "After being with the kids all day long, it didn't seem fair that I was always the one who got up with them at night and always the one who changed their diapers," Anna told me. "Yet I felt guilty for feeling that way and never said anything to Chuck."

It wasn't that Chuck was a selfish or bad husband or that Anna didn't thoroughly enjoy and value being a stay-at-home mom. In fact just the opposite was true. The problem was that they had both come from homes that were ruled by the "don't think," "don't talk" and "don't feel" rules, where the ideas, opinions and needs of the woman were clearly inferior to those of the men.

"At first I never expressed my needs to Chuck," Anna said, "because I don't think that I was even aware of them." As she started to become aware of them she tried to ignore them. When she could no longer ignore them she worked hard at spiritualizing them. "I really believed that if I was sincere enough and prayed hard enough the hurts and frustrations wouldn't bother me anymore." Her problem wasn't that she prayed, which was one of the healthiest things she had done. Her problem was that she stopped there and didn't put feet to her prayers.

"By the time I realized that I could no longer run away from my feelings it was almost too late." Anna and Chuck had become stuck in a relational rut and were well on their way to becoming married singles. Her health had gradually been getting worse and her doctors couldn't find any physical causes for her problems. Toward the end of our work together Anna remarked, "Looking back, now it's clear to me that my loving heavenly Father used my marital and physical problems to get my attention."

Although Anna had come for help dealing with her anger, that wasn't where we started to work. I started by helping her to establish a biblical foundation for who we are in Christ, what it means to be made in the image of God, what it means to have a personality and how God has designed our mind, will and emotions to work together in balance and harmony, and with some specific insights on our emotions. At this point she had the tools to begin to understand her God-given emotion of anger and to begin to change her deep-seated anger patterns.

I'd like to share with you some of the specific and practical steps God used to transform the role of anger in Anna's life. Anna learned that in order to change deep-seated anger patterns she needed to take some specific steps at three different times: (1) before she got angry, (2) while she was angry and (3) after she had been angry.

Before You Get Angry

The best time to deal with anger is *before* you get angry. Why? Because we need to learn how to seize opportunities to deal with discouraging, frustrating and painful situations *before* we reach the boiling point.

When you plan ahead, your perspective is less likely to be clouded by the intensity of your anger. If you wait until you are angry to try to understand and deal with the emotion, it is too late. Here are five important questions to ask yourself before you become aware of the fact that you are experiencing anger.

Is My Anger a Problem?

Just because you get angry once in a while doesn't mean that you have an anger problem. Anger is a God-given emotion that is a normal part of everyday life. So far we've seen that healthy anger has tremendous potential for good.

Anger only becomes a problem when we don't understand how to allow it to serve its God-intended function, and when we deny, suppress, repress, deny, stuff and ignore it. It becomes a problem when we allow ourselves to remain puppets of past patterns. It becomes a prob-

> *The best time to deal with anger is* before *you get angry.*

lem when we don't let it warn us before we're taken advantage of or even victimized. Anger definitely becomes a problem when it gets out of control and moves into more destructive emotions such as hostility, rage and aggression. In other words, anger is a problem when we haven't learned to express it in healthy and constructive ways.

What Are Some Indicators That I Might Be Angry?

We have seen that anger can come packaged in many different shapes and sizes. It can hide behind many different masks. Due to its negative reputation and people's tendency to deny it, anger could receive the award as the "Most Likely to Be Mislabeled" emotion.

This tendency is especially applicable to those with the cream puff anger style. Since Anna considered herself a "Certified Cream Puff," I encouraged her to make a copy of the word list found at the beginning of chapter 5 ("How Do You 'Do' Anger?"). For a two-week period, I asked Anna to put a check by each word that described what she was experiencing.

Anna found that for many years her anger had been disguised by terms such as "aggravated," "annoyed," "cranky," "exasperated," "grumpy," "out-of-sorts" and "touchy." This simple exercise showed her that whenever she experienced any of these feelings, she should recognize disguised anger.

When Am I Most Likely to Be Angry?

For two weeks Anna kept an Anger Log (discussed in chapter 6).

By faithfully using this simple tool she, for the first time, realized that there were certain times and situations that increased the likelihood that she would experience anger.

Anna discovered that she was most vulnerable during a two-hour period before and after preparing the evening meal, on Sunday mornings while trying to get the entire family ready for church on time, when Chuck would come home late without telling her, and when anyone in the family would not follow through on something she was counting on them doing.

By identifying these "danger zones" Anna could decrease the control of these situations over her emotional response. If this is the only suggestion you take in this chapter, I think that you will be surprised at how helpful it will be.

What's My Anger Pattern?

For many of us anger starts as a negative feeling toward something or someone. At the outset we need to learn how to take hold of that feeling and take the emotion of anger captive to the obedience of Christ.

Understanding your primary anger style points you in a healthy direction. Besides your anger style, it's also important to identify what your personal indicators are that you are getting angry. Sometimes we are the last one to know when we're angry. I have a friend whose dog knew he was angry before he did. When Allen would speak in a certain tone of voice his sheltie would put her head down and slink off into another room.

How do you know when you are getting angry? How do your children or your spouse know when you are getting angry? How do your friends know? Do you speak with a louder voice? Do you talk faster? Does your face get red or do your pupils get larger? Do you start to perspire? Do you have a churning sensation in your stomach? Do you feel like you want to throw or hit something? Do you want to run and hide? Does your body get more tense? Does your pulse increase? Is it more difficult for you to concentrate? Do you become increasingly preoccupied with what is making you angry?

We can learn how to be more effective in the future by better understanding the mistakes we have made in the past. Mistakes can be one of our greatest teachers, and since we've already made them and paid for them, there is no additional emotional cost for them. But it can cost us a lot not to!

The best way to identify your personal anger indicators is to look at your past experiences. Besides the Anger Log, it may be helpful to illustrate what you have discovered by drawing a bell-shaped curve. A sample is shown below. Next to the "road signs" on the front portion of the curve, you can place one of your personal anger indicators. The curve represents your anger and as the curve gets steeper the intensity of your anger

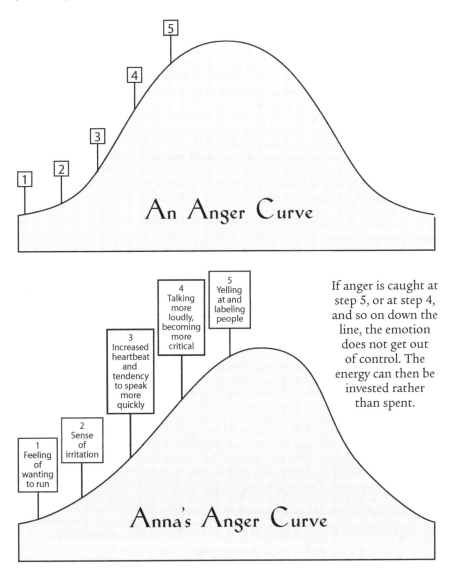

increases.

On Anna's curve her first personal anger indicator was the feeling of wanting to run. The next indicator was a sense of irritation. At this point she was aware of an increased heartbeat and a tendency to speak more quickly. By the time she reached the frustration level, she was also talking more loudly, was more negative and critical—and she was on her way to yelling and labeling people. After she had drawn her personal anger pattern, I encouraged her to keep a copy in her Bible. I suggested that each time she open the Word she glance at her illustration and offer a prayer of petition for God's help in dealing with her anger.

What Are the Benefits of Dealing with My Anger?

At this point it may be tempting to say to yourself, *Working on this anger stuff is a lot more work than I had anticipated. Is it really worth it?* Many people have found that one of the most helpful ways to answer that question is to remind themselves of the benefits of understanding and learning how to appropriately express their anger.

Hebrews 12:15 says, "See to it that no one misses the grace of God and that no bitter root grows up to cause trouble and defile many" (*NIV*). It is easy for a bitter root to grow up in our lives. Some people think they are doing the right thing by not dealing with or dwelling on the past, but there is a big difference between not dealing with the past and not dwelling on it.

We've asked many women, What are the benefits of dealing with your anger? Here are some of their answers:

Understanding and dealing with my anger has . . .
• enhanced by physical, emotional, mental and spiritual health.
• given me an increased source of energy to make the hard choices.
• improved my marriage.
• strengthened my relationships with my kids.
• alleviated my fear of someone else's anger.
• given my children a healthy model for this God-given emotion.
• helped me keep things in perspective.

- helped others better understand me.
- helped me clarify and protect personal boundaries.
- helped me to protect myself physically and emotionally.
- given me the power and courage to remove myself from the victim role.

When You Get Angry

As soon as you become aware of the fact that you are experiencing anger, you can ask five simple questions to help make this emotion work for you rather than against you.

Am I Willing to Acknowledge the Fact That I Am Angry?

This sounds so simple, but for many people it is easier said than done. Anna could easily say that she was aggravated, annoyed, cranky, exasperated, grumpy, out-of-sorts or touchy, but she hadn't been able to acknowledge that she was angry. "It's much more comfortable and acceptable for me to say I'm annoyed or grumpy than to say that I'm angry."

If you too find it difficult to say the "A" word (anger), you have a lot of company. You can work through this barrier by first silently acknowledging your anger to yourself. Then sometime when you are alone, you can say out loud to yourself, "I think I am angry" or "I'm angry!" feeling free to let your volume and tone of voice accurately reflect the intensity of your anger.

Admitting that we are angry sounds so simple, but for many of us it is easier said than done.

Lastly, find someone that you feel safe with and tell them about your anger. You'll find that the simple act of acknowledging and talking about your anger with someone will decrease your discomfort and fear.

It rarely helps to "try hard" to stop being angry. What does help is to acknowledge that you are angry, identify the root causes and redirect the energy away from attacking a person to attacking the problem.

Have I Put First Things First?

When dealing with emotional issues, it's tempting to find out what technique or gimmick someone else used and rush off to try, often in our own strength, to do the same thing. That's not going to work.

When I say "Put first things first," I mean that you should take it to the Lord in prayer. He created you and redeemed you and gave you His Spirit to help you do everything in His strength. Instead of turning on your husband or your children, turn your eyes on Jesus. Focus on what you do have, on your many blessings, on God's faithfulness and His many promises to you.

In 2 Corinthians 10:5, Paul exhorts us to take every thought captive to the obedience of Christ. We also need to get into the habit of taking every emotion captive to the obedience of Christ, especially the emotion of anger.

In Psalm 68:8, David wrote, "Trust in Him at all times, O people; Pour out your heart before Him; God is a refuge for us" (NASB). Go ahead, pour out your heart to God. Tell Him how you feel. Ask for His help and His guidance. It's foolish to try to do this in your own strength. In James 1:5 we are told that if we lack wisdom we only need to ask for it. In 1 Peter 5:7 we are told to cast all of our concerns on Him "because He cares for you" (NASB).

Many people have found the following simple prayer to be of help.

Dear Lord, Thank You for creating me in Your image with the ability to experience and express the emotion of anger. Although sin has damaged and distorted anger in my life, I thank You that You have promised to be at work within me both to will and to work for Your good pleasure. I thank You that You can cause all things to work together for good and that I can do all things through You who strengthen me. I ask You to help me to change my anger patterns. Help me to experience and express this emotion in ways that are good and that bring honor and glory to You. Amen.

What Are the Causes?

Notice that I said *causes*, plural. Anger rarely has only one cause; it usually results from a combination of factors. Remember that anger is almost always a secondary emotion. It may indicate that something is wrong with the decisions I am making or in the way I am allowing others to treat me.

When considering the possible causes of the anger it's important for us to rule out two categories of causes. First, we must make sure that our anger is not due to sin or selfishness. That's right! One of the main effects of sin is to make meeting our own needs, rather than doing God's will, the most important thing in the world. When we put ourselves first, we will inevitably end up last. When we put Him first (see Matt. 6:33), He will take care of everything else.

We are born selfish. We want what we want, and we want it when we want it. When we don't always get our way, when we aren't treated the way we think we should be, when we see others who get something we think we deserve, it is easy to get angry. If your anger is due to selfishness, identify it, confess it, seek forgiveness and ask the Holy Spirit for some practical steps to change that part of your life.

The second cause that is important for us to rule out is that of oversensitivity. If we allow ourselves to become oversensitive, anger can easily sound a false alarm. One of my good friends recently built a new home and had an alarm system installed. The first week they lived in the house, there were 11 false alarms. My friend finally discovered that the sensitivity levels of the alarm system were set too high. If our sensitivity levels are set too high, we can take offense when none is intended. We can look for slights when they aren't really there. We can assume the worst when it may not be true.

After you've ruled out sin, selfishness or oversensitivity, you are ready to learn how to identify the causes of your anger. At the beginning Anna found this to be a difficult step. It's not always easy to discern what might be causing our anger. However over time and with some faithful observation, record keeping and utilization of her Anger Log, Anna discovered that the primary sources of her anger were frustrations that she failed to deal with when they arose. "I kept on telling myself 'It's not that important!' when obviously it was." If you have kept the Anger Log, you already have a list of the most frequent and thus the most probable causes of your anger. For lists of categories, review the earlier chapters of this book.

In addition to identifying some specific causes for her anger, Anna also uncovered factors that increased her general vulnerability to frustration. These included physical exhaustion, especially the kind that resulted from high levels of stress. Another factor was the perfectionistic demands she placed on herself and others. She had been raised with the "enough is never enough" philosophy and so performance always fell short of expectations. One final factor that Anna identified related to basic gender issues. Anna stated, "I'm not a feminist, but at the same time it's frustrating to be treated as inferior, not very bright, an airhead or like a slave simply because I am a woman."

Your situation will be much different from Anna's. But the steps that God used to help Anna change her dysfunctional anger patterns can also be effective for you.

What Is the Healthiest Way for Me to Respond?

You are aware of the fact that you are angry, you have committed your situation to the Lord and you have identified at least a couple of the causes of your anger.

Now you must determine if there is anything that you can do. There are three kinds of situations in life: (1) situations I can control or change; (2) situations that I can influence; and (3) situations that I can do nothing about.

Don't increase your frustration (and thus your anger) by trying to change situations you can do nothing about. If your cause falls under this category, your only choice is to continue to give it to the Lord in prayer and turn your attention to things you can change or influence.

If it is a situation you can change or influence, get out a sheet of paper and make a list of your options. Don't worry about how practical your ideas are; just fill the sheet with as many constructive alternatives as you can think of. This may go slowly the first two or three times, but once you get the hang of it you may be surprised at how creative you can be.

If you've decided that a response is appropriate, determine whom you need to talk to, when to talk to them, how you can communicate in a way they are most likely to receive favorably and how long a time frame you have.

A good rule of thumb is to deal with a problem as soon as you become aware of it and have had time to choose how you can best express your feelings. Anger can vary in its intensity. If you are experiencing a mild anger, you can usually deal with the situation on the spot.

However, if the intensity of your anger is moderate to strong, it is usually wise to wait until you've taken time to think and pray it through. In Proverbs 16:32 we read, "He who is slow to anger is better than the mighty" (NASB). Why? Because the power and energy can be focused and directed.

God's Word clearly teaches that a patient spirit provides an opportunity for greater clarity and wisdom. To be "hasty in spirit" is similar to experiencing "vexation of spirit." To grow vexed or to become agitated in time of distress only makes matters worse.[1]

It is always best to express your anger at the source of your hurt. If you have bought into the myth that anger always destroys relationships, this may be difficult for you to do. The only way to pull the teeth out of that lion of fear is to do it. Challenge the misbelief. Risk speaking the truth in love.

Above all, choose to nurture a spirit of forgiveness. At some point we must choose to let go. I've worked with people who seemed to relish dwelling on the cause of their anger. But it's not enough to think forgiveness. Go to him or her and say "I'm angry and I'd like to tell you why because our relationship is important to me." If the other person isn't available or won't listen, write a letter stating and clarifying your feelings.

Now That I've Decided What to Do, Where Do I Begin?

Once you have decided that you need to communicate your anger and you have decided on a healthy way to express it, the next, and for many the most difficult, step is actually doing it. It helps to take the first step with someone you can trust. Anna decided that, while she experienced anger with a number of people, the best and safest person to begin to develop her new skills with was her husband Chuck. I would encourage you to find someone you can trust and start with her or him.

A few days after communicating her anger about a time he came home late, Anna went back to him. She reconfirmed her commitment to him to develop an increasingly healthy relationship. This helped both of them. It said, "Regardless of the surface struggles, you are important to me. My love and appreciation for you make the relationship worth working on, fighting for—and fighting about."

After You've Been Angry

Whether or not you successfully navigated those emotional rapids, you're not quite finished yet.

What have I learned from this experience? You must ask yourself this important question to complete the learning process. One of the best parts of being a Christian is that, whatever our experience, good or bad, we can learn from it with God's help. The longer you are a Christian, the more true you will find Romans 8:28 to be.

Discover all you can from your experience. Ask yourself these questions: What went well? What was different from usual? Were there any positive surprises? What could you have done differently? How were you able to see God's faithfulness?

Take Action

Draw a couple of blank anger curve illustrations and do one on yourself. Then have your spouse, child or friend do one on you.

ENDNOTES

Chapter One

1. M. Dittmann, "Anger Across the Gender Divide," *Monitor on Psychology,* 34 (March 2003), p. 52. http://www.apa.org/monitor (accessed August 2004).
2. A. Standen, "Getting Mad" (March 2000), http://salon.com (accessed August 2004).
3. This paragraph and the next are adapted from Gary J. Oliver and H. Norman Wright, *When Anger Hits Home: Taking Care of Your Anger Without Taking It Out on Your Family* (Chicago: Moody Publishers, 1992), p. 149.
4. Ibid., p. 209.
5. This and the next five paragraphs closely follow Gary J. Oliver and H. Norman Wright, *When Anger Hits Home,* pp. 20-21.
6. Matthew McKay; Peter D. Rogers; and Judith McKay, *When Anger Hurts* (Oakland, CA: New Harbinger Publications, 1989), pp. 207-225.
7. Kathy Olson, *Silent Pain* (Colorado Springs, CO: NavPress, 1992), pp. 11-13.
8. "Depression Strikes Women More," *Tyler Morning Telegraph,* December 12, 1990.
9. Kathy Olson, *Silent Pain* (Colorado Springs, CO: NavPress, 1992), pp. 62-63.

Chapter Two

1. Adapted by permission from an unpublished manuscript by an author who wishes to remain anonymous.
2. A. D. Lester, *The Angry Christian: A Theology for Care and Counseling* (Louisville, KY: Westminster John Knox Press, 2003), p. 85.
3. M. A. Preboth and S. Wright, "Women and Anger," *American Academy of Family Physicians,* with The Gale Group and LookSmart (March 1999). http://www.finarticles.com (accessed August 1004).
4. As quoted in Nancy Marx Better, "He vs. She," *Self* (June 1992).
5. Harriet Goldhor Lerner, *The Dance of Anger: A Woman's Guide to Changing the Patterns of Intimate Relationships* (New York: Harper & Row, 1985), p. 1.
6. Redford Williams, *The Trusting Heart: Great News About Type A Behavior* (New York: Times Books, 1989), pp. 165-175.

Chapter Three

1. M. Froese, "Women and Anger," *PageWise, Inc.,* 2002. http://meme.essortment.com/womenanger_rkjc.htm (accessed August 2004).
2. Dorothy C. Finkelhor, *How to Make Your Emotions Work for You* (Berkeley, CA: Medallion, 1973), pp. 23-24.
3. A. D. Lester, *The Angry Christian: A Theology for Care and Counseling* (Louisville, KY: Westminster John Knox Press, 2003), p. 37.
4. C. S. Lewis, *The Great Divorce* (New York: Macmillan Publishers, 1946, 1978), pp. 92-93.
5. Martha R. Bireda, "AACD Individual-Study Program," in *Love Addiction: Developing Emotional Independence* (Alexandria, VA: AACD, 1991), pp. 3-4.

6. Alice Isen, quoted in A. J. Hostetler, "Feeling Happy, Thinking Clearly," *APA Monitor*, pp. 6-7.
7. Stephanie A. Shields, quoted in Carol Tavris, ed., *Every Woman's Emotional Well-Being* (New York: Prentice-Hall, 1986), p. 131.

Chapter Four

1. Harriet Goldhor Lerner, *The Dance of Anger: A Woman's Guide to Changing the Patterns of Intimate Relationships* (New York: Harper & Row, 1985), p. 2.
2. Cited in Carol Tavris, *Anger: The Misunderstood Emotion* (New York: Simon & Schuster, 1983), pp. 181-182.
3. Carol Tavris, *The Mismeasure of Woman* (New York: Simon & Schuster, 1992), p. 263.
4. Harriet Goldhor Lerner, quoted in *Women in Therapy* (Northvale, NJ: Jason Aronson Publishers, 1988), p. 60.
5. Tavris, *Anger: The Misunderstood Emotion*, p. 180.

Chapter Five

1. "Women More Likely Than Men to Suppress Anger, Study Finds," *Denver Post*, 25 January 1989, sec. C, p. 4.
2. Susan Jacoby, "Why Is That Lady So Red in the Face?" *McCall's* (November 1983), pp. 123-124.
3. M. Dittmann, "Anger Across the Gender Divide," *Monitor on Psychology*, 34, March 2003, p. 52. http://www.apa.org/monitor (accessed August 2004).
4. Sonya Friedman, *Smart Cookies Don't Crumble: A Modern Woman's Guide to Living and Loving Her Own Life* (New York: Putnam, 1985), pp. 89-90.
5. Richard P. Walters, *Anger: Yours and Mine and What to Do About It* (Grand Rapids, MI: Zondervan Publishing House, 1981), pp. 17, 139.

Chapter Six

1. Gary J. Oliver and H. Norman Wright, *When Anger Hits Home: Taking Care of Your Anger Without Taking It Out on Your Family* (Chicago: Moody Publishers, 1992), pp. 91-124.
2. M. Dittmann, "Anger Across the Gender Divide," *Monitor on Psychology*, 34, March 2003, p. 52. http://www.apa.org/monitor (accessed August 2004).
3. D. C. Jack, "Understanding Women's Anger: A Description of Relational Patterns," *Health Care for Women International*, 22, 2001. http://web5.epnet.com (accessed August 2004).
4. Jon Tevlin, "Why Women Are Mad as Hell," *Glamour* (March 1992), p. 208.
5. Ibid., p. 209.
6. David Seamands, *Healing Grace* (Wheaton, IL: Victor, 1988), p. 168.
7. Paul Welter, *Family Problems and Predicaments* (Wheaton, IL: Tyndale House Publishers, 1977), p. 130.

Chapter Seven

1. Keith W. Sehnert, *Stress/Unstress* (Minneapolis, MN: Augsburn Publishing, 1981), pp. 74-75.
2. Georgia Witkin-Lanoil, *The Female Stress Syndrome: How to Recognize and Live with It*, 2nd ed. (New York: Newmarket Press, 1991), pp. 16-17.

3. Sheila West, *Beyond Chaos: Stress Relief for the Working Woman* (Colorado Springs, CO: NavPress, 1992), p. 104.
4. Ibid., pp. 106-107.
5. Witkin-Lanoil, *The Female Stress Syndrome*, pp. 125-126.
6. Ibid.
7. Keri Report, "The State of American Women Today" (Bristol-Meyer, 1991).
8. L. Dotto, *Losing Sleep* (New York: William-Morrow, 1990). A. T. Oafexis, "Drowsy America," *Time* (December 1990).
9. Ellen McGrath, *When Feeling Good Is Bad* (New York: Henry Holt, 1992), p. 206.
10. *Webster's Dictionary*, s.v. "perfect."
11. *Webster's Dictionary*, s.v. "excellence."
12. Report, "The State of American Women Today," pp. 132-133.
13. Ibid., p. 91.
14. Ibid., p. 102.
15. Lloyd John Ogilvie, *God's Best for Today* (Eugene, OR: Harvest House Publishers, 1981), Feb. 3 entry.

Chapter Eight

1. David Neff, "Christians Who Fear Too Much," *Christianity Today*, quoted in Carol Kent, *Tame Your Fears* (Colorado Springs, CO: NavPress, 1993), p. 25.
2. Gary J. Oliver, *Real Men Have Feelings, Too* (Chicago: Moody Publishers, 1993), pp. 80-81.
3. Earl Lee, *Recycled for Living* (Ventura, CA: Regal Books, 1973), p. 4.
4. Carol Kent, *Tame Your Fears* (Colorado Springs, CO: NavPress, 1993), pp. 22-27.
5. H. Norman Wright, *Afraid No More* (Wheaton, IL: Tyndale House Publishers, 1989), pp. 132-136.

Chapter Nine

1. Richard F. Berg., C.S.C., and Christine McCartney, *Depression and the Integrated Life* (New York: Alba House Books, 1981), pp. 34-35.
2. Archibald Hart, *Depression: Coping and Caring* (Arcadia, CA: Cope Publications, 1978), p. 22.
3. Ellen McGrath, *When Feeling Bad Is Good* (New York: Henry Holt, 1992), pp. 22-25.
4. Brenda Poinsett, *Understanding a Woman's Depression* (Wheaton, IL: Tyndale House Publishers, 1984), p. 17.
5. Ibid., pp. 82-87.
6. Ellen McGrath, et al., *Women and Depression: Risk Factor and Treatment Issues* (Washington, DC: American Psychological Association, 1990), pp. 34-39.
7. McGrath, *When Feeling Bad Is Good*, p. 2.
8. R. R. Fleve, *Moodswing* (New York: Bantam Dell Publishing Group, 1989), pp. 83-86.
9. M. Goed, *The Good News About Depression* (New York: Bantam Dell Publishing Group, 1986), pp. 195-203.

Chapter Ten

1. Susan Forward and Joan Torres, *Men Who Hate Women and the Women Who Love Them* (New York: Bantam Dell Publishing Group, 1986), p. 43.

2. Howard J. Parad and Libbie G. Parad, eds., *Crisis Intervention, Book 2: The Practitioner's Sourcebook for Brief Therapy* (Milwaukee, WI: Family Service America, 1990), p. 161.
3. Kathleen H. Hofeller, *Battered Women, Shattered Lives* (Palo Alto, CA: R & E Research Associates, 1983), n.p.
4. Parad and Parad, *Crisis Intervention*, p. 163.
5. Ibid., p. 167.
6. Forward and Torres, *Men Who Hate Women*, pp. 222-229.
7. William Petrocelli and Barbara Kate Repa, *Sexual Harassment on the Job* (Berkeley, CA: Nolo, 1992), 3/23.
8. Petrocelli and Repa, *Combatting Sexual Harassment: A Federal Worker's Guide* (pamphlet published by Federally Employed Women, Inc., 1991), 3/30.
9. Susan Webb, *Step Forward: Sexual Harassment in the Work Place: What You Need to Know* (New York: MasterMedia, 1991), pp. 96-101.

Chapter Eleven

1. Ronald T. Potter-Efron and Patricia S. Potter-Efron, *Anger, Alcoholism and Addiction: Treating Anger in a Chemical Dependency Setting* (New York: Norton, 1991), pp. 51-54.
2. Bobbie Reed, *When Pleasing You Is Destroying Me* (Dallas: Word, 1992).
3. Gerald W. Piaget, *Control Freaks: Who They Are and How to Stop Them from Running Your Life* (New York: Doubleday Books, 1991), pp. 154-55.
4. Piaget, *Control Freaks*, pp. 50-61.
5. Lloyd John Ogilvie, *Lord of the Impossible* (Nashville: Abingdon Press, 1984), pp. 129-130.

Chapter Twelve

1. Cited in Gayle Rosellini and Mark Worden, *Of Course You're Angry* (Center City, MN: Hazelden Publishing, 1985), p. 12.
2. A. D. Lester, *The Angry Christian: A Theology for Care and Counseling* (Louisville, KY: Westminster John Knox Press, 2003), p. 198.
3. Nancy Good, *How to Live with the Difficult Man You Love* (New York: St. Martin's Press, 1994), pp. 54-55.
4. Nancy Samalin, *Love and Anger: The Parental Dilemma* (New York: Penguin Viking, 1992), p. 5.
5. For different Christian perspectives on this issue, see James C. Dobson, *Straight Talk to Men and Their Wives* (Waco, TX: Word Books, 1980); John Piper and Wayne Grudem, eds., *Recovering Biblical Manhood and Womanhood: A Response to Evangelical Feminism* (Wheaton, IL: Crossway Books, 1991); Mary Stewart Van Leeuwen, *Gender and Grace: Love, Work and Parenting in a Changing World* (Downers Grove, IL: InterVarsity Press, 1990).
6. Interview with Deborah Tannen, *Bottom Line Personal* (March 15, 1991), p. 8.
7. Joan DeClaire, "The Importance of Understanding Gender Differences: Calling It Splits," *People Weekly* 38 (October 19, 1992), p. 131.

Chapter Thirteen

1. D. C. Jack, "Understanding Women's Anger: A Description of Relational Patterns," *Health Care for Women International*, 22 (2001), pp. 385-400. http://web5.epnet.com (accessed August 2004).

2. Ronald T. Potter-Efron and Patricia S. Potter-Efron, *Anger, Alcoholism and Addiction: Treating Anger in a Chemical Dependency Setting* (New York: Norton, 1991), pp. 39-41.

3. Ibid., pp. 85-101.

Chapter Fourteen

1. See H. C. Leupold, *Exposition of Ecclesiastes* (Grand Rapids, MI: Baker Books, 1978), pp. 154-155; and Franz Delitzsch, *Commentary on the Song of Songs and Ecclesiastes* (Grand Rapids, MI: Eerdmans Publishing, 1970), pp. 318-319.

SELECTED BIBLIOGRAPHY

Beck, James R., and David T. Moore. *Why Worry?* Grand Rapids, MI: Baker, 1994.

Chapman, G. *The Other Side of Love: Handling Anger in a Godly Way.* Chicago: Moody, 1999.

Cook, Kaye, and Lance Lee. *Man and Woman: Alone and Together.* Wheaton, IL: BridgePoint, 1992.

Davies, W. *Overcoming Irritability and Anger.* New York: New York University Press, 2001.

Kassinove, H., ed. *Anger Disorders: Definition, Diagnosis and Treatment.* Philadelphia: Taylor & Francis, 1995.

Kassinove, H., and R. C. Tafrate. *Anger Management: The Complete Treatment Guidebook for Practitioners.* Atascadero, CA: Impact, 2002.

Oliver, Gary J., and H. Norman Wright. *When Anger Hits Home: Taking Care of Your Anger Without Taking It Out on Your Family.* Chicago: Moody, 1992.

Paleg, K., and M. McKay. *When Anger Hurts Your Relationships.* Oakland, CA: New Harbinger, 2001.

Semmelroth, C., and D. Smith. *The Anger Habit: Proven Principles to Calm the Stormy Mind.* New York: Writers Showcase, 2000.

Tannen, Deborah. *You Just Don't Understand: Women and Men in Conversation.* New York: William Morrow, 1990.

West, Sheila. *Beyond Chaos: Stress Relief for the Working Woman.* Colorado Springs, CO: NavPress, 1992.

Wetzler, Scott. *Living with the Passive-Aggressive Man.* New York: Simon & Schuster, 1992.

Witkin-Lanoil, Georgia. *The Female Stress Syndrome: How to Recognize and Live with It.* 2d ed. New York: Newmarket, 1991.